# Everything But the Kitchen Skunk

*Ongoing Observations from a Working Poet*

*Poets notice what other people miss.
Nationally-known poet Molly Fisk's singular
perspective on love, death, grammar, lingerie,
small towns, and the natural world will get you
laughing, crying, and thinking.*

# Everything But the Kitchen Skunk

*Ongoing Observations from a Working Poet*

**Molly Fisk**

Story Street Press
Nevada City, California
2022

Published by Story Street Press
Nevada City, California
e-mail: mollyfisk@gmail.com
www.mollyfisk.com

This edition was produced for on-demand distribution by ingramspark.com
and createspace.com for Story Street Press.

*Cover design*: Maxima Kahn
*Cover photos*: Pascale Fusshoeller
*Cover skunks*: "Smarty" (front) and "Mama" (back), wild residents of Nevada
County, CA
*Author photo*: Aeron Miller Photography
*Typesetting*: Julie Valin/Self to Shelf Publishing
*Technical Support*: Clàudio Mendonça, Charlotte Peterson, Paul Emery,
Steve Baker
*Moral Support*: Nancy Shanteau, Julia Kelliher, Sarah Griscom, Sandy Frizzell,
Susanna Wilson, Jacquie Bellon
*Spiritual Support*: Scotts Flat Lake
*Financial Support*: Academy of American Poets Laureate Fellowship, 85
wonderful patrons, on and off Patreon
*Contributing Caffienation*: Three Forks Bakery & Brewing Co., Zuri Coffee Co.
*Original inspiration*: Carolyn Crane
*Frequency*: KVMR 89.5 FM Nevada City, CA (105.1 Truckee, 104.7 Woodland,
88.3 Placerville, kvmr.org), The California Report, KQED 88.5 FM San Francisco,
CA (89.3 Sacramento)

In some instances names have been changed to protect the innocent but most
of the time they remain unaltered to celebrate and encourage the guilty.

Printed in the United States of America

dedicated to

Jinny St. Goar
friend of my heart

&

KVMR
(FM Nevada City)
*music of the world,*
*voice of the community*

# Also by Molly Fisk

**Essays/Radio Commentary:**

*Naming Your Teeth*
*Houston, We Have a Possum*
*Using Your Turn Signal Promotes World Peace*
*Blow-Drying a Chicken*

**Poetry:**

*California Fire & Water: A Climate Crisis*
   *Anthology (editor)*
*The More Difficult Beauty*
*Listening to Winter*
*Terrain (co-author)*
*Salt Water Poems (letterpress)*

# CONTENTS

## Elbow Swimming

## Little House on Divisadero Street

## How to Count Flamingos

## Arizona Sunshine Lemon Pie

# ELBOW SWIMMING

## Praying for Possums

I live a fairly quiet life in a rural area and don't often feel visceral fear. Near-miss traffic accidents will shoot my adrenaline through the roof, or smoke from a wildfire that looks close, but by and large my days are uneventful, just the way I like them. Two years ago when the first possum marched in my open kitchen door, I thought that was high drama, especially since it kept running under the sofa instead of back out the door. *Ha! Little* did I know.

This summer there are no possums. However, last night I was sitting at my computer by the kitchen door, writing a poem. It was hot, still in the low 90s, and the door was wide open onto my deck. Various cats walked in and out, but I didn't pay much attention. At some point, the chewing sound coming from the cat food bowls four feet away sounded unusual. Possums have trained me to listen for irregularity in chewing patterns, but this didn't seem as loud as a possum.

I looked over in that direction, and my face went white. My body stayed perfectly still, but

I produced enough adrenaline to lift a Volkswagen bus over my head with one hand. It's a very strange sensation to have that much panic and electricity coursing through your body but not move a muscle. I took a few silent deep breaths and tried to relax my neck. Sid was pretending to be asleep on the desk, though I could tell he was watching. No other cats were in sight.

"My goodness," I said in a soothing voice. "You have a very fluffy tail, there!"

The skunk kept crunching his or her way through the first of two full bowls of Science Diet Hairball Control Formula for Seniors. "When is it," I asked rhetorically, "that skunks are most likely to spray?" Since I was already at the computer, and the skunk was clearly not leaving soon, I looked this up on Google, typing softly. Not that often, actually. Just when they are startled. Chomp, chomp. I let out my breath.

*"HIIISSSSSSSSS!!"* My head whipped around, the skunk whipped around and raised its tail to full height. Jack had arrived and was not happy to see his food being devoured. The three of us remained poised and motionless for long enough that my neck froze up again, and then the skunk turned back to eating and Jack jumped up and joined us on the desk. "Holy F-word," I said out loud, but serenely. "Don't do that again!"

We sat there, quite still, for what seemed like a few weeks, until the skunk took its pointy nose and beautiful tail back outside, pausing at the water bowl for a drink. I waited as long as I could stand it — about 90 seconds after the drinking sounds had stopped — and then got up to close the door. And lock it.

12 hours later, I am not recovered. I could probably still lift a Mazda Miata over my head. The screen door's been ordered. The cat door is locked. Please join me in praying that there's never a next time.

## That First Swim of Summer

Around here it went from cold and rainy to white hot in a matter of days, so some of us had to drive up to the lake and jump in, or in my case inch in, complaining all the while. My friend Sandy, who carried her wetsuit but decided she didn't need it, was her usual encouraging self, telling me how great it would feel afterward.

This makes no sense. There is no afterward, as any self-respecting Buddhist will tell you. There is only the present moment, when very cold water is entering your hoo-ha and about to freeze all your organs from the inside. I was once told that the phrase for this when it happens to men can be found by combining the first half of blueberries with the last half of basketballs, but according to a very reliable friend, this is quite wrong. So much for believing what you're told about other people's bodies.

But, I digress. We eventually got all the way in, swam around gleeful as newborn sharks, and then got out again. Sandy lay on the dock with Pat, who was smart enough to avoid swimming altogether, and I stood on the boat ramp kind of stunned. She was right, I did feel great and also smug. I was cool down to my bone marrow, a state that lasts for several hours and saves me from committing random heat-induced homicides.

The color of that lake is indescribable and every year on the first day we swim I go gaga over it and take a lot of pictures with my telephone. Then I get home and find that I have the exact same shots from last year and the year before that. There are only so many poses a lake can assume, after all. It's funny how completely you can forget about something you love so much. This year it had been seven months since we'd swum there. I can forget a lot in seven months, and more every year, it turns out.

For people of size, water is an exquisite medium. We float better than anyone else, so we feel accomplished and capable right from the start. We're held, gently, in the equilibrium between wet and dry without gravity to remind our bones that they're burdened, no heaviness — metaphoric or actual — to contend with. And it's the only time in our lives this happens. On land, we are clumsy mortals. In the lake, even when you swim as slowly as I do, we are gods. My physical buoyancy suddenly matches the mental state I try to maintain, and that coinciding feels a lot like joy. Maybe it is joy. In any case, it's hella fun and I can feel my

strength returning with every puny side stroke,
heading for the first buoy, and then the second.
Next week I will get to the third, and maybe even
the far beach, although I don't get out over there:
the Fisks do not like slimy lake edges. If I need to
rest I tread water and look around, pretending to
be a Canada goose, or float on my back hoping an
osprey will fly over me.

And sometimes, speaking of joy, one does.

## Fibs & Falsehoods

Today, I'm sorry to say, I told a lie to small children. It wasn't about Santa or the Easter Bunny. My lies are mostly original and have to do with the matter at hand. These two young boys, 5 and 9, were at my house with their dad, who was fixing the back deck. He had no childcare and I never volunteer as childcare, but I do often like kids and tend to want them to like me, which I arrange by giving them something to eat. I know this is wrong. But it works so well! Food and beverage bribery is an ancient art.

Yesterday when they showed up it was hot and I remembered I had two pomegranate popsicles left in my freezer. I keep popsicles around for emergency binge-ing when what I really want is coffee ice cream with caramel sauce, but that is another story. I asked their dad, who said *Sure*, and offered the treats, thereby becoming in everyone's eyes a nice lady.

Today, since the deck wasn't done, they came back, but I was out of popsicles. It's important to cement your lead. I stood around indoors for a

while mulling my options. It was too much work to
go to a store for more popsicles, I am not that interested in devotion. But I wanted to offer something.
There weren't any chocolate chips or mandarins
lying about, and somehow toast, which I regularly
feed to a 51-year-old when she comes over, didn't
seem to hit the right note.

Then I thought of the blueberries I froze last
week, for smoothies. Well, I said to myself. They're
almost popsicles, aren't they? Little teeny round
blue examples of the species?

I asked their dad again. It is poor planning to
incur the disapproval of your carpenter friends
over any subject at all, and people often have strict
food rules for their kids. He said, again, *Sure*, and
I brought out two little bowls of frozen blueberries.

*Did you know that frozen blueberries,* I said, un-
necessarily, *are how popsicles were invented?* The
oldest one looked up. *Blueberries come from Maine,
where they sometimes have freak snowstorms in the
summer.* This part is true, but extremely rare. *A
blueberry farmer went out at night to try to save his
crops during a snowstorm and tasted the berries to
see if they were still okay. They were frozen solid,
but also delicious!* I said, making it up as I went
along. *The farmer's name was Ned. He decided
frozen fruit would taste very good in summer, and
started an experiment. Apples weren't that great,
and oranges got so hard you'd break your teeth,*

*but orange **juice** turned out to be perfect. You can't eat juice out of your hand so he invented a mold to make the juice into a shape, and added a stick so it was easier to hold onto.*

*Cool*, said the younger kid, through purple-stained lips. *Do you have any more?*

If you're going to tell whoppers to an underage audience, the least you can do is give them all your blueberries.

*Sure*, I said.

## Opposable Thumbs

Sometimes I want to make something with my
bare hands so badly I think I'm going to go nuts.
I don't want to look at a screen, no matter how
enticing the comments or graphics. I don't want
to type or sit on a chair, I want the dance from
stove-top to cutting board to sink, from sewing
machine to ironing board and back. I want to
stand in a field and paint on canvas, or stand on
a ladder and paint the house. I want whatever
I do to make a big impact. Not one measly jar of
strawberry jam, but 20! Not the same color on
the house, but something new, bright, startling.
I want to begin and then finish, and have something to show for my time.

I don't know why this has gotten under my
skin today, but I'm feeling almost frantic about it.
For one thing, it's summer. Humans are supposed
to be outdoors. We were made to use our big thigh
muscles for miles of walking and our shoulders
for carrying things. What's the point of opposable
thumbs when all you do is hit the spacebar?!?

I think this has been building for a while.
First it stopped raining in my town, and the sun
came out. Then a few weeks later it got hot. The
usual summer stuff happened: flowers bloomed,
people took most of their clothes off. The girls are
swinging through town in their tan skin and short
skirts. The boys are shirtless — the muscles in
their arms stand out like twined pieces of rope. But
I've noticed that when they walk down the street
these days, a lot of them aren't looking around or
talking to each other. They're not even window-
shopping. They're gazing into cupped hands at
whatever is on their cell phone screen. It's bizarre,
and it makes them all look the same: the lowered
head, a little hunch in the shoulders, elbows bent
and thumbs working. It's not a young look, it's how
their middle-aged or older parents walk, whose
spines have started to curl with age. I can't stand it.

Usually when I've got a bee in my bonnet about
something, it's because there's an aspect that
applies to me. I think I'm finally feeling exhausted
from spending too much time on the computer. I
love the computer. I like the speed, the reach, the
way you can pop a photograph from your camera
onto Instagram in 38 seconds. I like the community I've tapped into through social media. But
something in me is feeling really lost.

In summer I sleep outdoors at night, and look at
the stars. Breezes come and go. The wisteria vine

on my deck sends out new tendrils overnight. I can feel the temperature cooling and then warming up again. The Dipper makes its slow circle around the North star. It's been such a wet, cold year, I've only been out there for two weeks. But I think sleeping without walls has slowed me down again and reminded me of who I am. A human animal. Someone whose body was designed to interact with the world. Even though I hunt and gather at Grocery Outlet instead of the veldt, I still thump melons to see if they're ripe yet, and smell the milk to figure out whether it's gone bad.

Without intending to, I've let the computer steal my body and now I want it back. It's time to find a you-pick strawberry field and get moving.

## Oh, Happy Day

Today is my birthday, and believe it or not, I am turning 65. Since I don't believe it, there's no reason you have to either. It's entirely unbelievable. This is what happens when you aren't paying attention... you fold a little laundry, feed the cats, and wash that favorite green plate for the thousand-and-twelfth time — looking out the window above your kitchen sink to see if any baseball-bat-sized zucchinis are gazing back at you from the vegetable garden — and then *whammo*, only five minutes later, you're old.

One thing old people do, in my experience, is give random advice to anyone who will listen, and even to some who won't. I am looking forward to this very much, even though as a poet and also as a life coach, I give a lot of advice already. It is just so much fun, I am glad to have an excuse to give more of it!

Here's a sample for you: Wear your gol darn mask, please! I'm in the demographic of people who probably won't live through Covid-19, and if you end up being the chowderhead who

thought mask-wearing was a government plot and
breathed on me, resulting in my death, it is not
going to be pretty. Not only will I haunt you for the
rest of your sorry and ignorant life, but my numer-
ous Facebook friends and Twitter followers, not to
mention all cats everywhere, will do their best to
ruin whatever you try to accomplish. If you think
this is a curse in addition to advice, you are smarter
than you look.

Another thing, while we're at it. Curb your
dang wheels when you park on a hill! As I drive up
Broad St., my town's main drag, at least half the
cars have not curbed their wheels at all, and another
five or ten have curbed them the wrong way, so if
the brakes fail the cars will go rolling into the middle of the street and cream some poor tourist trying
to take a photo of our quaint Victorian rooftops.
If common sense and care for your fellow humans
doesn't move you to learn this, maybe the $40 ticket
will help. And it is a question on the California
driving test, by the way.

While we're discussing things that endanger
everyone, how about that handy lever on the left
side of your steering wheel? I named an entire
book to try to get people to use turn signals, but as
far as I can tell it has not helped at all. Who decided
you were the King of Siam and didn't have to drive
safely? Your mother? Your fraternity brothers? Get
a grip! Do you wear a seatbelt? Do you stop at stop

signs? Jeez Louise, I don't know where you people come from. The planet of you're-still-a-baby-and-everyone-else-will-clean-up-after-you? The childishness involved here is astonishing. I don't know who the heck you think is in charge of the world, but it happens to be you, Buster. One of the seven billion.

Whew! That was great! I feel a decade younger at least. There's nothing like just saying it. As a newly old person, I look forward to you breathing into your mask and me getting many more years of becoming a curmudgeon.

## Elbow Swimming

For people of my vintage, there's an awful lot
of talk about how to age well, better, slowly, with
grace, on a budget, and so on. Two suggestions in-
volve learning new things and getting exercise, so,
being an efficient old poet, I thought I'd combine
them. Not that I pay attention to the wheedling
of advertisements or the moralistic warnings of
most health articles. When you weigh as much as
I do, it's better for your blood pressure to avoid
these arenas, and I am always looking out for my
health.

I swim a lot in the summer. Not the Olympics
kind, with kick turns and mighty lung action.
The Canada goose kind: where you go along at
a decorous pace looking queenly with your head
above water and your feet scrabbling below the
surface. I say I go up to this lake for its turquoise
color and the ospreys, both of which I want to see
from water level. This is not the whole truth. The
whole truth is that my mother hated getting her
face in the water, I have no idea why, and as a
good daughter, I copied her.

Now I'm middle-aged, Mom's gone, and I envy
people who swim "free-style." Secretly in my own
mind I call this "elbow swimming," because of
the beauty of that homely joint when people pull
their arms out and then thrust them back into the
water. This stroke seems graceful, powerful, and
when I've tried it, impossible. My memories from
Paul Daly's Swim School in Corte Madera are dim,
although I learned it there when I was 9. I can
breast stroke for miles, but when it comes time to
lower my face and breathe to the side, a lot of desperate coughing ensues.

I asked my friend Sandy to teach me to do this
as a birthday present. She rose brilliantly to the
task, but it took me a while to gather the requisite
props. Bathing cap, goggles, a snorkel, and then
later I needed a clip because despite the snorkel I
kept breathing through my nose. We tried this in a
swimming pool with some success, and then I was
instructed to practice.

The gear is in my car. When I go up to the lake
every day I leave it in the back seat and do not
practice. One problem is I can't get the bathing
cap on: Sandy had to help me in the pool. Don't
laugh. I can hear you laughing. OK, fine, laugh, I
don't care. I am being denied longevity by a rubber
hat. No, it's not too small, it's the big size for long
hair. Another friend suggested I skip the cap and
just tie my hair back. She reminded me the pain of

learning doesn't last, but I hate not being good at something everyone else can do. Plus, I am going to look *so* ridiculous. And I will probably drown.

However, I am determined to give my elbows a chance. Even if there are gruesome things under the water that I will wish I had not seen. Even if an osprey tries to lift me out by the snorkel, mistaking it for a neon pink trout. One of these days, I will bring all the props down to the dock and put them on.

I think I'll start around 10 p.m., when it's truly dark and no one can see me, though.

## Plum Tuckered Out

The thing about living in the country, even when you're not any kind of farmer, is that things ripen and then are ready to be picked or to fall, and there isn't a darn thing you can do about it. I'm looking at a sink filled with yellow plums. Not counting the two stock pots on the stove and the three quarts of plum flesh I've already processed, I have a big basket of them on the counter, probably another basket's worth on the tree, and I've given four bags to friends. We're entering the hottest week of the year and the only hours I can bear to cook are between midnight and 6 a.m.

This is absurd. I mean sometimes it's fun: I like picking fruit and boiling it up and listening to the jars ping when they seal. But I really hate pressure and crazy amounts of fruit on every tree is a lesson in pressure. Plus, I have a life and a day job! I can't be up making preserves in the middle of the night. The plums, however, do not care. They ripen, they fall on the driveway, they rot. I can't stand the waste, when I could be making beautiful golden jam to give everyone for Christmas.

After the plums, my farming life calms down. I
can tomato sauce and make pesto to freeze for winter,
but I get the tomatoes and basil at the farmer's
market, so I have some control over the amount
and timing. My next emergency fruit adventure
will be in late September when the pears ripen.
Thank God the county road crew ripped out my
persimmon tree when they widened the road for
bicycle lanes, or I'd be going insane over those in
September, too. I don't have enough friends to give
all this largesse, either. Probably, for the pears,
I'll call our county's gleaners, kind people who
come and pick everything left on a tree for the
Food Bank and our local homeless shelter. 50
pears is going to be plenty for me, and the tree
produces hundreds.

I didn't plant these trees, I inherited them,
and I can see there are illusions attached to the
situation that could bear examining. *My* illusions,
or possibly *de*-lusions. One is that not harvesting
edible food is morally wrong, even if you can't
consume it yourself. Another is that in those Little
House on the Prairie books by Laura Ingalls Wilder,
everyone was having fun while putting up food
for winter. Pa played his banjo at night, the girls
peered into cast iron kettles until the syrup was
just the right color, it looked elemental and virtuous.

I also blame Martha Stewart. Those recipes
and photographs we drooled over! Let me just say

that millionaire media moguls baking their own bread in a state-of-the-art kitchen as a phalanx of professional gardeners weed her lavender beds is not truth in advertising. Me, elbow deep in plums, winkling out the pits with my bare hands at three in the morning while wearing a decrepit Lanz nightgown is truth in advertising. With an elderly cat trying to sleep on the stove top the whole time.

I think we need a reality show about that, to spare innocent urbanites from thinking this home canning nonsense is a good idea.

## Carefree

The older I get, the saner I feel, which is a
little odd. I'm not someone who ever felt actively
insane, but I definitely had moments, sometimes
months, of frustration and instability. I got dreadfully thrown by bad love affairs, and refused or
was unable to leave a few unkind men to the
point that close friends began to mutter about
dissolving our friendships.

Now when I eavesdrop on younger women
in cafés I marvel at the amount of drama they
describe, and laugh at myself that I could have
forgotten the intensity of living with all those
hormones. It's fun to listen in for a while, but then
I get distracted and go back to what I was doing.
I don't have much bandwidth for novels, either,
with their intricate social commentary.

Plenty of articles describe how age changes us
— I won't bore you with a list you either already
know, being older, or probably won't believe, being
younger. What's interesting is that though the
world is falling apart all around us in so many
ways, I feel so calm about it. At this time last year

I was a wreck, hiding from Covid germs, tracking every wildfire in seven western states not to mention my part of California. This year, I'm astonishingly chill.

A friend thinks we're just burned out on worry and fear, floating along in an unrealistic stupor. Maybe. I can see her point. But I also feel like an observer looking down at climate crisis and so much uncertainty as from a great height, about as distant as the rings of Saturn. Not being a billionaire, I'm not launching myself into space to check out this theory of dispassion. I'm making plum jam instead, an earthly pursuit whose cost/benefit ratio is overwhelmingly better than space travel, ask anyone. And feeling steady of hand and heart as I stir up the plums with sugar and cardamom, boil the little jars and glasses.

You just never know, do you? There is, in age and experience, a kind of pleasant relinquishing. Stuff drops away that you didn't know you were holding onto in the first place. Things that were potent turn out to be way past their sell-by date.

This same friend got her eyelashes dyed the other day. I'd completely forgotten I used to do this, too. I thought it made my eyes look more vivid, being a redhead with invisible lashes. One of the nicer ex-boyfriends used to examine my face carefully afterward (he was an artist) and say that it really did look as though two large black spiders had landed on my eyelids. He loved it in the way people love the paintings of Salvador Dali, with the melted clocks, etcetera. So much for seduction.

My life coach is a great one for saying, "Well, either it will or it won't," and then smiling at me. She has beautiful pearly teeth and isn't even 50 yet. I think this philosophy has finally sunk in. I don't feel apathetic; it's not a lack of caring. It's some new version of carefree. My grandmother, whose 115th birthday it is today, by the way, used to shrug in her later years when asked about the larger sort of household repairs she was facing.

"Oh, well," she'd grin. "I just figure *laissez heir*..."

## It Takes a Train to Cry

My first venture out of town in four months (because of the pandemic) was like an acid trip. Five in the morning, so the light was pale and it was blessedly cool. I made my own coffee and got on the freeway — mostly a two-lane for the first half hour, thank God, so I could practice. I live in the trees and my eyes were so unused to seeing wider views that they kept lingering on them too long. My car kept slowing down and I had to keep reminding myself to give it gas.

Since March I've been driving only five to ten miles around town, and then when summer started, I added the wild and crazy 15 up to the lake. But a friend had taken the train to see her first grandchild and on the way back from Portland to Denver had a four-hour layover in Sacramento. A friend of 45 years.

There's a new shopping mall at Lake of the Pines that was only bare dirt last time I passed. I've never heard of Holiday Market, its anchor store. This is not exactly like having Martians land in a nearby field, but it's surprisingly close.

By 6 a.m., there was some commute traffic. I kept
taking the exits just before everything stopped,
which made me feel lucky but was also a little
otherworldly. I didn't dare turn on the radio — the
visual disorientation was already too much for me.
I didn't even see my friend as I pulled up at the
train station though she was smiling and waving
and then had to run after my car. And that was
its own miracle of displacement — such a familiar face, but not on either of our own turf and her
hair's really white now. We masked up and she
rode in my SUV's back seat, windows down, to Fox
& Goose, a breakfast place my Facebook friends
had recommended.

   After we were seated, I notice a statue and said,
"Look, there's a large bronze duck!" She kindly
pointed out it might be the Goose of the restaurant's name, so I was spared the embarrassment of
adding "and a pig!" in reference to the other statue,
on second look clearly a fox. As I say, I was sort of
hallucinating.

   Temperatures in Sacramento have been in the
triple digits for weeks, but at 7 a.m. in the shade
without sweaters, we were freezing. The Twilight
Zone theme song ran through my head. Listening
to Ellen's tales of grandparenthood and Covid train
precautions, not to mention bits and pieces of her
labor law cases, brought me down to earth again,
finally. And the goat cheese omelet helped, too.

Three hours later, when I had to get back on the road, my eyes were completely in focus and I remembered the shortcut I like to take that cuts out four stoplights on the way home. I did cry, watching this dear friend not turn and wave as she walked toward the California Zephyr. She hates prolonged goodbyes and over the years I've learned to give her just a quick "I love you." We can't hug, anyway.

I wouldn't say that I wallow, but I can get weepy, especially now all bets are off and who knows when any of us will see each other again. Also, as we know from Bob Dylan:

"It takes a lot to laugh, it takes a train to cry."

## Beets & Raspberries

I don't have anything coherent to say but I
know it's good for me to write, like walking is,
and beets. Beets are very healthy, though I don't
always feel like eating them and I haven't cooked
one in years. The magenta flesh, raw or cooked,
stains my cutting boards. In Vermont, as kids
in summer, my cousin Liz and I would paint our
cheeks with each half of a beet before dinner.
Heaven knows where the other six kids were...
Our moms and grandmother trying to put supper on
the table and the fathers off somewhere, Grand-
pa reading a newspaper in his chair. Mosquitoes,
evening rain, the grass so green it made your eyes
hurt. I'm still not that fond of shucking corn. The
famous slam of a screen door hitting the frame
but more often than not it caught your Achilles
tendon on the way out. I'm not nostalgic for most
of that heritage, although I miss the smell of Sea
& Ski. Proust via Smith-Kline Pharmaceuticals.
I think I inherited my love of the Vermont house
from my mother — inherited isn't the right word,
it's like that new thing where we carry trauma

our forebears went through only it isn't bad, it's their longing for the summer before we were born. I can almost feel the crush my mother had on Ethan Bisbee even into adulthood, when I truly can't remember the names of all the men I've slept with myself.

Does that happen to you? Do you suddenly wake up one day, your front teeth half-way into a raspberry, and think, "I don't even like this stupid fruit! I'm from California, what I love are blackberries and fresh figs!" I didn't grow up picking raspberries in the early morning before the bears got them. Good lord. How much of our lives are wasted on not understanding who we are? And the tidal pull of unsatisfied mothers. Truly, I could weep.

But I won't. I have already wept plenty about that and more. I didn't plan to stop crying but I kind of have — not even a rush visit to the vet yesterday with my extremely old dying cat opened the faucet. His face was swollen on one side, the same side my mother's was swollen on, in fact, when she was dying. I've never had to put an animal down; usually they disappear and I assume are eaten. It's hard to tell which is worse, watching or having them vanish, because all of death is equally worse. Losing my dad to a mid-morning heart attack from 3000 miles away was not better than listening to my mom's ragged breathing from the next room and wondering if it was ever going to stop.

   Now I cry mostly in solidarity, as with the
friend on her front step who was terrified by
a recent pro-Trump mob in our town and still
shaking with fear. Tears rolled down our respec-
tive cheeks where we stood, the requisite six feet
of social distance between us, perhaps the same
way they've rinsed the faces of terrorized humans
for centuries. This sort of empathy is something
most people carry inside ourselves intact, trans-
generationally and across cultures, too.

   Like love. Or the taste of some sweet juicy
summer fruit, your mother's favorite.

## Middle-Aged Mermaids

Have you ever gone to water aerobics? This is just what it sounds like: an exercise class that raises your heart rate, held in a swimming pool. It's perceived to be for older people, particularly older women, whose joints maybe can't handle a hard workout on a gym floor. And it's true, the class I go to has 10 or 12 women over 60 in it. But it also has 5 or 6 women under 60, and 2 or 3 men. It may be easier on the joints than other, land-based classes, but it doesn't have to be easy. You can make it as hard as you like. I come out of that blue water pretty tired, and after a month I can see my shoulder muscles again.

But the reason to go to water aerobics is not the exercise, nor even the cool water on a scorching day. It's not the dark green pines and cedars that gradually give their shade to the evening participants. The reason to go is because it's hilarious, and laughing is so good for us.

At 6:00 p.m., all the small humans get herded out of the pool, dried off, and escorted home for dinner. The decibel level is reduced by half, even

though 20 somewhat raucous adults are now
walking rib-deep through the water, first "like
Barbie" (on our tiptoes) and then "like Ken" (on our
heels). As the hour progresses, we jog, cross-coun-
try ski, do myriad versions of jumping jacks, and
pick invisible peaches with one hand while putting
them in a metaphoric basket with the other and
simultaneously kicking our own bottoms with our
feet. We take styrofoam barbells into deep water
and scissor, flutter, and frog kick while emulating
a pendulum.

We do crunches and stretch our obliques (whatever they are) while attempting not to drown.
We perform amazing feats using only a so-called
"noodle," bicycling around the deep end like de-
mented mermaids. It's so completely ridiculous,
and our leader is so enthusiastic, that the time
flies by — just when your sides are truly sore from
too much laughter, it's over.

Then there's a little cool-down stretching back
in the shallow end, and we disperse across town
into our own lives, energized and used up in equal
measure, full of camaraderie and delirium.

I usually end up at the grocery store — having
forgotten to buy cat food, again — not dripping exactly, but my hair riotous and my dress damp over
the bathing suit. Ordinarily, this would be embar-
rassing, but I have so many endolphins coursing

through my bloodstream I don't care what anyone thinks of me, I'm just glad to be alive.

I want you to be glad to be alive, too. Life is hard and getting harder. Next time you don't know what to do with yourself, find a lake or ocean or public pool. Don't worry about the exercise part, even though it's good for you. What you're looking for is buoyancy: an hour of non-stop chuckles in the water.

## I'm Not Nervous At All

My house cleaner is coming over tomorrow
morning for her once-a-month attack and I'm
dashing around the place trying to get things out
of the way so she can actually see the counter tops
and floor in order to clean them. I know you know
what I mean. Some people laugh and say *Why are
you cleaning up, isn't that what the cleaner is supposed to do?* These people are not thinking clearly
or else they have daily household help.

I'm not cleaning, I'm tidying! There's a huge
difference. Tidying means putting all the laundry into the basket. Cleaning is vacuuming the
now-visible floor. I'm the only person who can do
this job easily, since I tossed the clothes toward
the basket in the first place, so I know these are
dirty and the red sweater next to them is something a cat pushed off my bureau and is perfectly
clean. I also know the Christmas Decoration box
lives under my bed and my house cleaner would
have to ask, which takes too much time, and I
won't be here to answer, I'll be over at the hospital having an echocardiogram. It's possible some

of the energy I'm expending on ferocious tidying is due to this appointment.

Bodies are so weird, really. I mean, back in the day I could have told you exactly when I was ovulating every single month. There'd be a little pinched feeling and then kind of a *ping*, as if a marble had dropped, on one side or the other. And yet, I had no idea, 12 years ago, that one of my arteries was 80% blocked. None! After I got home from the hospital we had a very serious talk, my circonflex artery and I. *Why the hell didn't you tell me?!? I could have done something so much sooner! You almost got us into big trouble here, what's the deal?*

Silence. Not a peep. I was *so* outraged. I see this in my cancer students all the time, too. The feeling of betrayal when you find out you've been leading an ordinary life, driving carpools and paying taxes and your OWN BODY has secretly been having cancer behind your back. The shock of not knowing is almost as bad as the illness.

I've taken out the recycling, done the dishes, and put that clean red sweater in its bureau drawer. This is also the moment I search the house for heretofore undiscovered cat barf. If I have any house shame, it's about the constant regurgitation taking place around me and the thought that someone else will find it first and decide I am a slob. I sort of am a slob but I really don't want anyone to find out. A slob who would rather not end up staying in the hospital tomorrow, but at least her house will be clean.

Have you ever had an echocardiogram? They make you walk on a treadmill wearing very few clothes and say encouraging things while at the same time deviously increasing the grade. Just when you can't go one more step you have to fling yourself onto a table to be slapped with electrodes and measured every which way. It is not, let me tell you, for the faint of heart.

I hope I'm OK, I really do. No one else is going to put up with all these antique cats.

## That River in Egypt

Right now this minute it is cool enough to sit outside, and not smoky. The meat bees are still asleep and haven't begun dive-bombing the remains of my breakfast. Outside on this restaurant's patio, the conversation is humming along: no one's too loud or playing some damn video on their phone with the sound up. There is sun and shade, there are songbirds I can't identify, the freeway sounds a lot like the ocean in its random surgings and quietings.

It's confusing to live in a world where so much is at stake but your own life in the moment on a Thursday morning feels serene. Yes, there's a mask on my table and I don't shop after nine in the morning. People I love have died, but not people I know well. Love from a distance, like John Prine and Julie's dad.

Most humans are not all that good at abstract thinking. Of course the mathematicians and philosophers are out there, and maybe get more airtime than your average dentist or UPS driver, so we hear more from them than their numbers warrant. But humans, by and large, are sensory animals and react to immediate pleasures or threat. On a day like today, I can barely remember how bad the smoke was last week. I'm still surrounded by wildfires but since they're getting a handle on those big ones, we don't hear the planes overhead or see panic in our news feeds. I can't smell any smoke.

Someone wrote recently somewhere — maybe *The Guardian* — that this is what he expected with the climate crisis: people would only begin to take action when they themselves had lost a home to fire or been up to their own waist in a flooded New York subway car. When their parents were dying of Covid and they had to say goodbye on Facetime. This, of course, is a real problem when we should have cut off use of fossil fuels eight years ago, or twenty, in order to survive. I feel like I'm watching an ocean liner finally come to a stop and begin to turn around, in that achingly slow way they do, so huge and ungainly, but the storm clouds are already massed overhead and the tsunami visible on the horizon. We're watching this from the liner's deck, not the shore, of course, because in this metaphor there is no shore.

Some people say, "Don't talk like that, its so depressing! You have to have hope." I say *Wake the hell up and smell the coffee, the roses, whatever you can still smell in case you don't have Covid your-*

*self.* Hope is what you muster up after you've faced reality. Before then, what you're experiencing is denial.

And denial isn't unreasonable, to be fair. It's one of the common responses to terror. It helps the human brain not get completely overwhelmed. But it's not useful when you're problem-solving quick action at an enormous scale. It's not something to encourage in others just so you won't feel lonely. It's a temporary strategy.

As I was writing, my friend the fire-fighter of 41 years sat down at the next table. We talked for a while about this phenomenon. He said, "people are sleep-walking through Armageddon."

# LITTLE HOUSE ON
# DIVISADERO STREET

## The Practice of Practice

Today, all I want to do is amble around town
and photograph gloriously-colored trees, scuffling
my feet in their fallen leaves. As you know, we had
a hot, smoky September and most of October, when
it seemed as though fall color was never going to
happen. Then, after three cold nights, all the trees
turned at once, fast and spectacularly. Rain is
forecast for tomorrow, so their beauty, as all beauty, is fleeting. I teach on Thursdays but I'm going
to sneak out of my schedule for part of the day and
absorb the crimson, peach, tangerine, pumpkin,
fig, and sunshine-colored leaves.

As a poet, really I should put things like this
on my calendar. Writers traffic in sensory images
and visual ones are primary, at least for West-
erners. I'm always telling my students to practice
the others in order to enrich their work — smell
things, taste them, close their eyes and listen. I
hesitate to give you advice — well, that's not true,
I love giving advice, it makes me very happy. But
right now, with everyone uncertain and tender,
so full of emotion from the swirling world, I don't

want to burden you with anything more. But I will say that, when life is overwhelming, it soothes me to consider whatever is directly in front of me. This frog's extremely loud voice, which seems to be coming from behind the refrigerator. How a teacup's handle attaches to the bowl. The way a zinnia's petals — the last zinnia of summer from my unkempt yard — overlap in circles around its yellow center. Even the symmetry of hubcaps can give me a jolt of pleasure as I'm walking down the street under these Technicolor leaves.

I had to practice looking closely, because I have by nature a big-picture mind. I was the one in school who could connect the farthest dots and thought the small stuff wasn't worth noticing. This is how writing helped me grow up. To get better at it, I had to avoid my own tendencies and move in new directions where I was inexpert. That took years to learn, since I am also by nature somewhat rebellious and surly, almost always convinced I'm right. These traits take patience to dismantle.

But I wanted to write well more than I wanted to prove anything to anyone. I learned to tolerate not being good at things long enough to become better at them. I found out that practice really works and to keep going won't kill me. In this way I have improved my writing, broadened and strengthened my compassion, and taught myself how to tolerate swimming in very cold water, something else I plan to do today, even though it is, God help us, November.

Looking closely is a great tool for setting aside politics and despair, which are both abstractions. Finding something concrete to examine pulls you into the present moment, which is, after all, where we live, and where we're going to keep on living no matter who wins or loses any given election. Go ahead: take a look at your socks, or your left thumbnail, or the light filtering through that maple out your window and the way it angles in and stripes the floor.

## Bohemian

I can never remember whether we're supposed to bake things for longer at this altitude than the recipes says, or less long. I've only lived here for 25 years, and I've baked something at least once a month, except in the summer when it's too hot to turn on the stove.

My grandmother, born in 1906, baked every day. She didn't believe in buying things you can make. She also didn't believe in going to anyone's house for dinner without zucchini bread or a tin of home-made oatmeal cookies as a hostess gift. She lived on Cape Cod, so altitude adjustments weren't involved.

When was the last time you said "hostess gift" in a sentence? Which is, of course, class-related. I don't say it either but I certainly heard it growing up. We were admonished regularly to say "hello" or "goodbye" and "thank you" to the hostess when arriving at or leaving someone's house. The host could go suck eggs, apparently. He never got any credit, and perhaps rightly so, since all men did in the '50s in this demographic was mix cocktails and earn money. The women deserved all the credit for inviting the guests, wrapping Chinese water chestnuts in bacon, making deviled eggs, and emptying cans of oversalted Planter's Peanuts into cute little wooden bowls. And that was just for a cocktail party. Never mind Beef Wellington and Baked Alaska. Plus, of course, cleaning the house before and afterward. My grandmother, being female, knew the score.

We came from a class of people who did not employ cooks, although cleaning ladies arrived once or twice a week to help our mothers. This was useful, but it didn't save the woman of the house, who usually had four children under the age of seven, from tearing out her hair on the day of a party. People we knew had cooks, or had their parties catered, and other people we knew never threw anything but potlucks, which in the '50s were considered quite Bohemian. Anything the least bit innovative was called Bohemian in a certain tone of voice which meant you'd better not go there or be that way or you were going to hear about it later. Code.

I'm delighted to tell you I turned out entirely Bohemian, but it took a while. Despite going to the right college and dating four different men who had "the third" at the end of their names, I managed to escape quite a bit of my class trajectory. (As did some of those men; you can't judge a book by its cover.)

But we can't escape our families of origin completely, which is why I mentioned the altitude adjustment. The timer just rang, telling me the banana bread I'm making to take to a friend's house tonight might be ready. This is the recipe's timing, from the good old Bohemian *Moosewood Cookbook.* According to my calculations, it will either be overdone, underdone, or perfect. I will write down which it is on page 193, so I know for next time, breaking another class taboo that one not deface books unless you're the author who is signing them. I don't know if this will be a hostess gift or eaten on the spot as potluck.

Part of the fun of being Bohemian is creating a sense of mystery.

## Gala, Winesap, Ruby Crisp

I'm sitting at the kitchen table of a dear friend, listening to her practice the piano: scales and then some Mozart, I think a rondeau. She's not a professional, but an amateur who's taken lessons for decades from the same teacher in New York City. We're an hour north of there up the Hudson River in Beacon, New York.

Forty-five years into our friendship, we've both landed in towns of about 15,000 (in my case, Nevada City and Grass Valley combined). My 22 years in Nevada County differs from her two years in Beacon, and California is not New York, but there are similarities — the social problems of homelessness and zoning to manage growth. The artsy little stores that come and go. We have recreational tourism and Beacon has proximity to museums (Storm King and the Dia Foundation) and the Culinary Institute of America. We each have a river and a primary agricultural crop: marijuana in Nevada County, apples in the Hudson Valley. The weather right now is the same, too — alternating

rain and snow with sometimes an hour of sunshine
to keep us from losing our minds.

One of the great pleasures of long-time friendship is perspective. Under the layers of job changes
and child-rearing, now grandchildren, different
kitchen tables, the person you knew at 18 is still
there, ready to talk about anything you can
think to say, cocking her head as she considers
a question, her beautiful eyebrows lifting, her
hands describing graceful shapes in the air. I
don't remember what sparked it yesterday, but
we laughed so hard in a deli another customer
asked what was going on.

Nothing, and everything. That's the perspective
part. Whatever is happening now will change —
all the details are incidental but also completely
beautiful and sort of the point. If you don't register
the little stuff, what are you seeing, really? This
is my question to myself. Marketing and religion,
economics, are all invisible. You notice the closed
storefront that held baby consignment wares last
week, the new bare-root apple trees bundled in
sheaves of Gala, Winesap, Ruby Crisp. You see the
lines on your friend's face and the white hair curl-
ing into her husband's collar and think, *Wow, this
is real! Somehow we got older.*

My friend is at the piano, wearing, incongruous-
ly, black socks with white musical notes on them,
which strikes me as hilarious. Last night she

stuffed a chicken with the Meyer lemons I brought her, and six of us sat around the table talking about the state of the world, climate change, aging in place, glass-blowing as a career, and how small towns choose their mayors.

I should maybe care more about choosing a mayor, but let's face it, I just don't. I care about whether my friend is content with her life, and how the scent of lemons braids itself with garlic and rosemary in the gathering dark.

# Wheel Within a Wheel

Yesterday, as I drove out the long driveway,
Joe was discing the field where my friends
will plant their next 8000 apple trees, and
turning up rocks and more rocks. This is New
York's Hudson Valley, known for its apples. My
friends have built a new house with rocks from
the property, collected over two summers by
their sons and many helpers. When I first saw
the house I thought of Tuscany and southern
France, but after driving around the extended
neighborhood and seeing some old American
stone houses made just the same way, I realized
theirs fit perfectly into both the natural and the
historic landscape.

Then I drove five hours, stopping along the
way to pay my respects to the graves of my father,
his parents, and grandparents. It took me forever
to find them, as the Fisks have flat granite headstones close to the ground and it's the other family
name, Bradley, that you can see on a big monu-
ment, which I'd forgotten.

This morning, I'm in northern Vermont sitting at a café's outdoor table next to one of the famous, ubiquitous Vermont stone walls. A different kind of stone: gray, flatter, and dry-stacked, where the stones in New York were honey-colored and seemed rounder. Not actually round, but nothing like flat. And though they might be granite also, the family headstones were whiter and sparklier.

I'm awash in personal history, even though David Byrne is singing through the open café windows and Waitsfield, VT — which I haven't seen in 25 years — is now a crazy tourist town full of Pilates and glass-blowing studios and so-called folk art galleries that sell sappy-looking wooden cats. Cutesiness has never been my aesthetic, especially not here, where my mother's father bought an old farm in 1935. It was old then and is a lot older now. Never winterized, and only electrified in the 1970s, it was the refuge and oasis for my mother and her sister every summer of their lives. I came often when I lived in the East, well into my thirties.

I'm having so many feelings there's no way to describe them to you, so instead I'll tell you about this flower I'm looking at on the other side of the stone wall. Over five feet tall, growing in a clump of about 20, with sturdy green stalks so they don't fall over and long oval opposite leaves. Its head is umbrel, which means lots of little flowers looking

like one big flower (think of an umbrella), and it's
a purple close to pink and not too bright: a faded,
soothing color. Its name, mysteriously, is Joe
Pyeweed — Pye is spelled P–Y–E — which made
my mother giggle. I would sometimes use this
name on my return address when I sent letters
from Cambridge to her in California. She loved
California in the end, but its dry climate wasn't
her favorite. She was so happy here, in the fertile,
wet, green Vermont summers picking raspberries
and washing her children's hair in the kitchen
sink — there still is no hot water heater so we use
tea kettles — surrounded by stone walls, birches,
sugar maples, ancient drooping cedars, Black-
Eyed Susans, Queen Anne's Lace, and Mr. Joseph
Pyeweed.

## You Got It

I'm sitting on my sofa in early sunlight. There's
a frog warbling out the open door, some cars
whooshing past, and a very old irritated cat on my
right knee, stabbing me affectionately with claws
she can no longer retract. I would say life is good,
and I will say it: Life is good. Even though the
power is out again and some day soon I'm going to
have to bury this cat and her brother in the yard,
which I'm not looking forward to. Seamus and An-
gus and Red Jack and Ajax are already out there—
hit by cars on the road before I built the cat fence.
Max, too, who died of something his mom caught
in the shelter. Oliver, Sprocket, Jerry, Ivan, and
Bella, the most beautiful of them all, disappeared
so I never dug graves. One of old age and the rest
from predation, I assume.

This week a friend reminded me that we don't
get what we want and we don't get what we need:
we get what we get. This is, as we used to say, a
bummer. But there's a way that facing reality head
on can feel good. I didn't get kids, I got cats. So
I love cats and don't have to try to make enough

money to send them to college. We live in danger-
ous fire terrain, so we get blackouts and hope we
don't get a horrendous fire. I'm not saying action
is useless — I've been acting plenty to reduce my
neighborhood's risk and be as safe as I can, to
change the kinds of power we use and elect saner
people to office. But right now it's Thursday and I
have no juice, so I'm coping: writing this commentary by hand in a notebook. I'm thankful my friend
has a suitor who brought her a generator last time
we lost power, and I can stay in her guest room
and use my breathing machine at night.

I'm not saying you shouldn't be cranky or
grief-stricken by what you get — some of what
happens is horrible, just look at the Kurds this
week or the ten thousand acres burning today in
Sonoma. We feel how we feel about all of it. But
at a certain point it's useful to keep going and do
what you can, whatever that is. Line up to buy
more gas for the generator. Cancel the reading you
had scheduled. Wash your hair in the sink.

I've spent a lot of my life begrudging things that
happened or didn't happen, and letting all that go
was a wonderful thing. I'm not the famousest poet,
the most perfect friend, the slenderest anything.
But here I am, regardless. After the last outage I
had to throw away gallons of soup I'd just made for
winter. I was furious and then exhausted. What's

the point of trying to take care of ourselves when this happens?

And now it's happened again! Insert your favorite swear word here.

This afternoon I went swimming with friends, out to the middle of Scotts Flat Lake since no one was there and we wouldn't get run over by random motor boats. The black oaks are turning yellow on the hills. It was gorgeous.

You get what you get.

Congratulations, I'm sorry, and best of luck.

## What We Get

Watching a TV show last night made me want
to get married. Something about the ending being
tragic and exquisitely well done, not the stupid,
hollow, melodramatic finales we usually see, but
simple and devastating. I woke this morning from
a dream in which I was holding someone's hand.

When I say, "get married," that's not what I
actually mean — it's my generation's code for "be
in a long-term committed partnership with someone I love," which is too long to say. I have many
thoughts about literal marriage and most are un-
complimentary. I don't need to go into them here.
But what it might mean to hold someone's hand
— the knuckles and pads of the fingers familiar,
comforting, the expanse of palm — to feel that
casual and meaningful human connection again
seemed precious to me, who hasn't thought about
holding hands in years.

Life is incredibly complicated. I should proba-
bly just end here, right? You know what I mean.
Everything has background, context and history.
People don't know themselves or know all too

well. We build our lives, alone and together, we change, fail and succeed, make do, make hay while the sun shines, hurt and care for each other. All the things — the great big human mess.

I'm not telling you which TV show: I don't want to spoil it. But in a hospital hallway, exhausted, one character asks another to marry him. They're sitting in those awful molded plastic bucket chairs that are welded together in groups of four like industrial church pews, so they're side by side, not able to turn toward each other. It's unexpected in the plot and far from any idealized proposal scenario. Neither of them is beautiful, or young. It's a minor scene, between a main character and an ancillary one, and doesn't last long. She asks if he's serious and he says "completely." She leans back in her chair and after a pause turns her head toward him and says something like, "Yeah" or "Okay."

I loved how ordinary it was, stripped of romance but loaded with feeling, coming from someone who maybe had thought about proposing but wasn't ready or wasn't sure or hadn't had time to plan it yet. It was so symbolic, blurted out like that... probably why it moved me so much.

Maybe we're all in a hospital hallway right now, not waiting out a surgery on someone we love but caught in that same vivid mix of uncertainty, dread, realistic prognosis, and hope-against-hope. The climate, the fires, the virus, the future. And

I'm suddenly thinking I don't want to do this alone,
even though I've been alone for ages, even though I
already briefly sort of had a love-of-my-life and are
we allowed more than one?

Lately I hear people saying, and I've even said
it myself: *We don't get what we want, or what we
deserve. We get what we get.*

Today this seems both true and over-simplified.
What if we don't see what we have? What are we
not recognizing that's right beside us? And what if
we get what we ask for?

What then?

## Deer Heart

Since the pandemic began, some days I never leave my house except to go swimming up at the lake. I never even wear earrings any more, because they snag in my mask. But yesterday was different: yesterday I went out three times — once to the bank, once to a physical therapist to learn more about vertigo, and once to go swimming. Three outings meant that I passed a dead deer on the highway six times. I didn't see the deer itself until the third pass because it was lying off the pavement in the weeds. What I saw, what you couldn't avoid seeing, was the huge organ all by itself in the bicycle lane.

At first I thought it was a heart, even though I knew it was too big. It would have had to belong to an elephant at that size, or a giraffe, none of which we have around these parts. But it had a heart-like aspect — like a beef heart at the butcher's, not a valentine. It was almost the size of a soccer ball.

It was also intact each time I passed, no crows or vultures pulling it apart, no obvious gore. As if it had just fallen out of the back of a truck. There was something mysterious and iconic about the way it remained there, unmolested.

The fourth time I went past I thought, *I should take a picture of whatever that is*, but I had to be somewhere. This isn't like me: I'm not usually an examiner of roadkill, I'm too squeamish. But writers are curious, it's an essential part of our job. Finally, on my last traverse, with a wet bathing suit under my dress, I stopped. Two young guys were examining the scene also and told me it was not a heart but a stomach. *We're trackers*, they said. *We teach tracking*. My neighborhood is like this. *I'm a poet*, I answered.

They showed me where the deer was likely crossing from and to — an old animal trail established before the invention of asphalt. We couldn't figure out by looking at the deer how the stomach got out of the body. There was some blood in its nether regions but no hole to be seen, and very little blood on the road. One tracker had thought it could be a uterus but the deer was male. We didn't try turning it over. The other tracker lightly touched the animal's cheek and then they took off. I got some photographs.

Whenever I see roadkill I resolve to sell my car and become a vegetarian. I feel angry, frustrated, sad, and helpless. Sometimes I cry. I hate humans

for a while, every last one of us. Then, as is inevi-
table, I go back to my life.

I've learned to drive more slowly at dusk on this
two-lane highway near my home. Only a couple of
days ago I avoided hitting a deer myself that was
standing on the white line about to cross. I felt
lucky after the adrenaline had dissipated.

Maybe it was the same deer, or the mate or the
sister of this one in the weeds.

Maybe it was the reincarnation of someone I
loved.

## Have You Thought About Joining the Peace Corps?

Whenever her adult children got restive or seemed to be at loose ends, not sure what to do next with their lives, my mother could be relied on to suggest we should join the Peace Corps. This was at first irritating, and then boring, and then hilarious, in the way that family stories or habits turn out to be riotously funny because they're so predictable. None of my siblings nor I had any interest in the Peace Corps. It did not cross our minds. Travel, sure. Helping other people, fine. We were usually wrestling with what kinds of jobs we wanted to do or where we should live, sometimes trying to work around a partner's life goals, too. Joining the Peace Corps was too extreme a solution. Go ahead and blow up your life, it seemed say, and then see what happens.

I've met quite a few people, all of them about ten years older than I, who did join the Peace Corps, and found it incredibly valuable. A friend's mother did after she'd retired from being a high school French teacher in Maine, and had a wonderful time somewhere in Africa that I've forgotten, where both her French and her teaching came in handy. My mom was the person who should have joined the Peace Corps, just as she should have become a doctor instead of, or in addition to, having four children and making smocked dresses and little shirts that matched her own. She ended up becoming a counselor in a learning disabilities clinic and then in her fifties went to nursing school. Although she liked this work, her hearing was getting bad by then and rolling the bodies of head-injured Hells Angels over in bed kind of wrecked her back. By the time I'd gotten smart enough to say *she* was the one who should join the Peace Corps, she wasn't healthy enough, in her view. The moment had passed.

I haven't had children, as you may recall, so I'm not able to give anyone advice about raising them. I've watched the world go by for six decades, though, and have observed a lot of humans. The happiest ones I've seen are those who figured out what they wanted to do and then did it. Yes, I'm white and middle-class and had a privileged vantage point as well as a blinkered view of mostly people like myself. And yes, the men had a much easier time of this than the women. But given those contexts, it was still pretty clear that if someone had a wish or drive or propensity for something, and followed it, they carried an aura of contentment other people did not.

Sometimes these trajectories don't last. I was a sweater designer for ten years and really loved it. In year eleven, though, I got bored. I feel incredibly lucky to have found a second creative life as a writer, something I backed into rather than pursuing and after 30 years am not bored with yet. There is luck and privilege all over the place in these matters, but there's also an important core question: What do you want? It's not easy to answer, and it changes. But keep your eye on it.

Who knows? Maybe you'll be the one who ends up joining the Peace Corps. Check it out at www.peacecorps.gov

Toni Fisk would be so proud of you.

## Forget John Wayne

It's been six months since the pandemic hit and I'm finally gathering my wits. I've been in three bad car accidents in my life, and this feels like a similar process except the recovery after a car crash is shorter and they don't happen to everyone in the world at the same time. I guess it's just shock, on a large scale.

In many British police shows, the survivor of a crime sits on the fender of an ambulance wrapped in a blanket, being given a cup of very sweet tea. I don't know why sugar helps with shock but it's the unvarying remedy. And you know the British and their tea. The victim sits there, stunned, in the middle of a lot of action — people measuring things, taking photos, conferring with superiors. You get the feeling that solutions will be found.

The Covid-19 pandemic situation in the U.S. doesn't have this sense of purpose attached to it. We're all sitting on ambulance fenders in shock, looking around but there is no tea. This isn't entirely fair: plenty of people are out there developing vaccines and making more ventilators out

of used Ford pick-up mufflers. The instantaneous-
ness of mask production and selling was a sight to
behold. And any event this new, global, and deadly
was going to be chaotic at first. But it's a lot worse
than it had to be.

I don't think about leadership much. I live
alone and work for myself. When something needs
to get done I'm the one who has to do it or find
someone else to do it. I don't feel particularly *led*,
even though I vote and stop at stop signs. There's
no leader in my daily life, like a boss or a bossy
spouse. There's no one around it would occur to me
to follow; I don't even have to negotiate.

But watching the Keystone Kops display that is
our country's response to the pandemic has been
eye-opening. How much it would have mattered
to have a plan already in place, to have the sup-
plies we needed available. Many good things have
been done by individuals but as I watch the whole
picture, it's easy to see how much more effective it
would be to have someone in authority say, *Wear
a mask*, and *Don't go to spring break*, as well as
*Hang in there, we can do this*. A leader.

This mess is the American Dream in action.
Independence, when you look at the examples, is
almost always a move away from existing order
into chaos and the experience of dealing with that
chaos on your own. It's a great story, but it is a
story, our national myth — it's not real. People

don't survive alone. Sure, John Wayne rides into the sunset. The movies never show you the next week when he runs out of coffee and stops by a friendly-looking ranch to borrow more. When his horse throws a shoe, he has to find a blacksmith. What's true is that all those racist, patriarchal, solitary heroes either went mad or froze to death. They got bucked off their palominos and lay there on the trail with two broken legs until the wolves found them.

It was the townsfolk who survived: growing gardens, starting schools. Bringing sweet tea when someone was in trouble. Taking care of each other. And, leaving the movies behind, the indigenous people who lived on that same land before us, taking care of each other.

Think about it.

## Little House on Divisadero

I feel as though I just discovered a pot of gold at the end of the rainbow, but it's only a hippie coffee shop with good lattes and great light. It isn't even new — I've been here several times before. But I guess someone was running an antique store inside it, along with the café, and he moved out, so the drapes and heavy dark furniture are gone, leaving motley chairs at pale round yard sale oak tables and sun streaming in. The baristas are friendly, and I have a new pen with which I am writing these sentences down that is a beautiful forest green.

It's possible, if you are a fairly confident person, to think you know what's going on in your own town. All I can say is *HA!* Fat chance. Even if you've kept track of the three new breweries and the Mediterranean joint on Mill St.'s soft opening, you've probably missed something, unless you issue the county's building permits. People are moving here and hatching schemes at a great rate. I'm not sure we have enough customers for all these new eateries, especially in winter, but time will tell, and I've already proved I don't know what's going on.

This month I have a new book out: my fourth compilation of radio essays like this one. I gave a reading from it the other night and during the Q and A afterwards, a long-time resident of Nevada County piped up and said: "I want to live in *your* town!" We all guffawed, but I know what she means. Sometimes even I want to live in the town I talk about on the radio, and not that other place where there's no parking on Broad St., people have to sleep outside on rainy nights, and we have a terrible meth problem.

Thus can literature beguile us. At a different reading from the new book, again during the Q and A, someone asked what I was working on now, and I described the book about a pioneer couple that is currently driving me crazy. I am 50 poems into it and still don't know what's going on.

"Why pioneers?" she asked.

"Probably because of Laura Ingalls Wilder," I said. "I'm the oldest of four kids so I heard all nine of those Little House books read aloud in the living room, one after the other, four separate times. I used to make floor plans of log cabins, figuring out where the furniture would go, and rag dolls with calico dresses and yarn for hair. I was kind of obsessed."

Then my sister, who was in the audience, raised her hand. This can be a precarious moment for a writer, as you might imagine, and I did feel myself stiffen up a little as I called on her. You never know if you're about to get busted in public for some important factual error.

Sarah said, "Once, when we were little girls, Molly came into the kitchen and asked our mother if we could move Out West."

Everyone cracked up, including me, because we were born and raised in San Francisco.

## Phoebe & Miles

Sometimes when I think something is hard, or is going to be hard, I avoid it. I mentioned this to a friend and she laughed: "You and everyone else on the planet!" which I confess startled me. We are each the hot centers of our own galaxies, after all, and now and then it shows.

Accidentally over the last 15 years, I've written a hundred poems about a young couple who move from Oregon to California in 1875. Their parents crossed the country in covered wagons, but they were born in the west. This is kind of what happened to me although my parents were in a Volkswagen bug convertible.

I never planned to write about pioneers — a woman's voice just came to me and I wrote her thoughts down, originally in poems. For a while it seemed this thing was trying to be a novel, so I took out the line breaks and made the stanzas into paragraphs. But in that form I felt I had to have the piece make more sense. Part of what I like about poetry is all the empty space involved. You don't lead the reader by the hand as much, you let her have her own reactions and make her own connections.

The other thing about novels is they're supposed to have a conflict and then resolve it. This doesn't work for me: I hate conflict. I didn't want anything bad to happen to Phoebe and Miles while they were in my care, and that stopped me writing for a couple of years.

Then I missed them and returned to the book, put all the paragraphs back into stanzas saying "I'm a poet, gosh darn it!" and wrote some more. Phoebe got pregnant, as one did so regularly in the 1800s, and Miles got stung by a wasp at one point, and later contracted the flu and was temporarily debilitated and quite grumpy. That's all the conflict I can stand. No one will die in this book, or run off with a Pony Express rider. I omitted most of the social strife of the era, too, from which my characters are far removed, living in the Surprise Valley, in California's northeast corner.

I'm slightly embarrassed by the story, to tell you the truth. Leaving out conflict makes it seem a bit sentimental. It contains two sex scenes that I won't be reading aloud in public. But Miles and Phoebe are insistent that I finish it.

Now I'm doing the last big job of cleaning up the chronology. When you write poems, or when I write poems, I just write what I want, I don't worry about anything outside the poem. This has led to some hilarity like Phoebe canning pears in August when they don't actually ripen until late September, as well as being in her second trimester of pregnancy both in May and in October. I think this is called "continuity" in the film industry. It's a pain in the neck, but understandably necessary. I hate to see glaring inaccuracies when I'm reading something — it makes me distrust the writer.

I would like to be trusted at least, if not adored, and am launching myself into this last bit of hard work today. Writing about it here has been a nice way to procrastinate though, and I thank you for listening.

## For the Love of Mike Ditka

I just wrote a really bad poem about the origins of those phrases with names in them: *Oh, for Pete's sake* and *Heavens to Betsy!* Wikipedia didn't have much useful to say except first names can often be a substitution for "God" when you don't want to upset people who might be offended if you take His or Her name in vain. I understand this with a phrase like *Oh, for God's sake*, but I'm not sure who would say *Heavens to God!* I don't run in God-mentioning circles, but I know whenever I visit Boulder, Utah, my friends there remind me that hearing "God" spoken in an unreligious way is worse for the locals than hearing those stronger terms we use that I can't voice here on the radio without being fined. Trying to keep it to *darn, dang, drat, oh fudge,* etc. is preferable.

Personally, I've always imagined it was Pete Seeger's sake I was invoking, a man of conscience and heart who did so much good in the world despite playing the banjo. In situations like this, I think one is allowed to substitute any Pete you'd like. The politician involved in transportation who

just adopted twins, the former controversial base-
ball player with a flowery last name, that musician
who led all the children out of Hamlin, anybody.
As far as Betsy goes, Wikipedia thinks Betsy Ross
might have been the original model, but they're
just making that up.

I love language and its weird turns of phrase,
its oddball constructions. But predictably, I love
the old fashioned stuff, the things I heard as a
child, as when my grandmother used to tell us
not to play too vigorously on a local hill, lest we
go "end over tea kettle!" I knew what my end was,
but always wondered which part of me was the tea
kettle. I still wonder this.

I'm not as fond of the modern day constructions.
This week a horrible word has come into my sights:
Shacket. I saw it in a women's clothing catalog,
then on a website, and later my social media-savvy
friends confirmed it for me. It's been around for at
least a year but until now I've been spared. What?
I thought. *Shack* as in decrepit tool shed? Some
sort of *shared racket*?

*Shacket* is an amalgamation of Shirt and Jacket. This item used to be called a shirt-jacket, which
to my ear is plenty short and has no need of further abbreviation. Who the heck even talks about
these things? Of course, it's all marketing. You
can't just re-peddle clothing styles every ten years
any more, now you have to rename them as fur-

ther proof they're exciting and not some dumb thing
your parents wore to do yard work in the Connecticut suburbs. That oversized LL Bean shirt over a
turtleneck in milder fall weather is not a Shacket.
Now you need to purchase, at ten times the price,
something that looks just like it from Neiman Marcus or Dior.

For the love of Mike, how can anyone possibly
believe capitalism isn't a shell game?! *Shacket*,
indeed. And when I say Mike, of course, I mean
former Chicago Bears football coach Mike Ditka.

## 56 Degrees

Right now I'm sitting on my sofa wearing a mask. A friend has come over to write with me, and this is our winter indoors protocol. We are both masked and both writing, the front door is cracked open, and she's ten feet across the living room in a leather chair that creaks when she shifts her weight, like a Western saddle. It's raining.

I would not invite just anyone into my house. I'm essentially in a pod, as they say — like peas? Like whales? — of one. But I have some friends I see more often than everyone else and she's one of them. We've swum every day for six months in a nearby lake and yesterday it finally got too cold for me, not even worth the bragging rights, so I invited her over to start a new tradition right away. This isolation business is no joke and I don't want to lose my sanity.

It's fun writing with someone else. Not as much fun as swimming, but also companionable, and very productive. We don't converse, we say hello, get tea or glasses of water, set the timer for 25 minutes, and write. I'm writing this, as you can

hear, and she's writing something about cold water
swimming suggested by *The New York Times*.
They don't take everything she sends them, but
they like her work. KVMR merely asks me not to
say things that will close down the station and
incur big fines. More than once, I've written about
our lake, but since cold water swimming is getting
trendy in the news I may have to stop. There's
nothing I hate more than being "on trend." And
it's everywhere, from profiles of octogenarians who
swim year round on the Icelandic coast to pieces
promising cold swimming will protect you from dementia. Everyone loved that octopus movie, where
the guy's free-diving in 48 degree water!

I don't mind being protected from dementia,
but that's not why I watch Labor Day disappear
behind my shoulders, and then Halloween. Swimming is summer fun and heat relief, a beautiful
landscape just 10 miles from home, and it fulfills
the anger-management function that keeps me
from biting people in the jugular vein when they
misbehave. After a swim, I'm the nicest you'll
ever know me. Blissed out, optimistic, benevo-
lent, relaxed. It's a miracle.

I want to hang on to those feelings, as anyone
would, and luckily have another friend who's been
swimming until December for years. Last fall she
dragged me with her, day after day, which is the
only way this works, you have to keep going — if

you miss a week you can't stand how cold it got. It was so bizarre and unlikely for me to walk into the lake in just my bathing suit when the water was 63 degrees, then 61... At 59, it took on a kind of magic. I had no plan except to see how it felt tomorrow. We made it almost to Thanksgiving, when a week of rain and 58 degree water finally won.

This year my writer friend joined us, and we've had a blast. But yesterday the lake was 56. I lost all feeling between my toes and the rest of my skin felt hot and prickly, the way those freezing cures for warts used to feel in the 1960s. My shoulders said to me, quietly, "Molly, we've had enough."

My body doesn't ask me for much, and it's carried me for miles through that beautiful teal-green water.

It seems only fair after all these years to be accommodating.

# HOW TO COUNT FLAMINGOS

# #MeThree

I'm feeling torn today about whether to bring up the #metoo movement, or to avoid the subject. I've been public about my own abuse experience since 1991, which was 26 years ago.

Aren't the Christmas lights fabulous this year? People seem much more enthusiastic about holiday self-expression than usual. And around here, the vast migrations of geese and swans to the flooded rice fields of California's Central Valley are over-whelmingly gorgeous.

In 1991, I began writing and talking about the incest I had experienced, and was pretty much shunned. Some people in my family said I'd always been a liar. A friend from grad school dumped me, saying she couldn't handle the drama. One of my brothers was afraid to leave me alone with his baby daughter, as if I were the perp and not a victim.

I like the geese, but it's the swans I go to see every year. Their combination of beauty and grace with awkward goofiness pierces my heart. The flooded fields are shallow, so a bird will look like

it's floating, a vision of long-necked elegance, and
then suddenly stand up to lumber a few yards on
clumsy webbed feet. This makes me giggle: the
illusion, the reality, the combination.

Outside my family, a few close friends stood
by me, but I was mostly met with silence. After
every poetry reading, though, at least one person
would come up to tell me her story, to thank me for
speaking out. That still happens, all these years
later, even though I don't often read poems about
abuse any more. People tell me I saved their lives.

The other thing that's lovely about swans is
how, on a sunny day, they will lift off one field and
fly to another, turning in flight and seeming to disappear. You look at seven or eight of them against
the blue sky and then they vanish before your very
eyes, angling their bodies somehow. A moment later there they are, necks stretched long and wings
flung out, their big creamy breasts lit like clouds.

After my memories came back, I gained 100 lbs.
I still carry it, mostly in my torso. From the side, in
the mirror, I almost look pregnant, and sometimes
I wonder what this quarter-century gestation is
going to produce. Sometimes I search for midwives.
Sometimes I think that this is my scar. Without
the weight, people might think I am fine, and I
might vanish back into the life I led before, the
life of good grades, prompt thank you notes, judge-

ment, self-sacrifice, and a mysterious underlying volcanic layer of rage.

What's been hardest to learn is how to hold the idea of "both." My father: wonderful, funny, smart, full of love — and a criminal, a child molester. My family: wonderful, funny, endearing — many of whom still don't believe me. You could crack up trying to hold both. People do. People kill themselves because it's so hard. Or they give up and choose one side, denying the other, which is how our culture behaves: pushing the subject underground for decades after a brief airing.

Would you like to drive down to Marysville and visit the swans with me one of these days? I usually go alone, but this seems like a good year to have company.

## Storytelling

At a coffee shop this morning, my friend Joe
said he had two great stories, and I waved him
over. He told me about a roadkill beaver he picked
up on the freeway near Kingvale last week, where
snow was piled twelve feet high. Not just any beaver, an 80 lb. beaver, the size of a bear cub. I had
no idea they got that big! Someone Joe knew had
seen it and wanted the tail, don't ask me why. We
discussed getting more squeamish in our middle
years, and how a person creates his or her own
interesting life by saying "sure" when asked to do
favors for friends like fetch a dead beaver from
the side of the road.

His next story involved retrieval, too: a truck
tire from a flooded field in the Central Valley, late
at night in pouring rain. There was also an old
refrigerator in which a skunk had taken shelter.
The skunk popped out to look at Joe as he rolled
the tire past, but did not spray, and then went
back into the fridge again. Since skunks enter my
house through the cat door searching for kibble

and I talk about it on social media, these days people bring me their skunk stories.

Sometimes, at coffee shops, I am actually trying to write. Today I was getting over laryngitis and not in a hurry, mostly glad to be out of the house, not contagious any more and desperate for a latte. I wasn't looking for stories, but I was available to hear them. Storytelling is how humans learn. Understanding a narrative arc is wired into our brains. The beginning, middle, and end, maybe a moral if there is one, maybe just being transported to another place for a minute helps us take things in.

Recently NPR aired a piece about how the Inuit, who are busy trying to survive in their landscape, don't have time to be angry. "Anger's not going to solve your problem," said one of the speakers. "It's just going to stop you from doing something you need to get done." This influences their parenting style: instead of yelling and giving kids time-outs, they steer their behavior with stories. This makes for a lot of cool-headed kids. Another speaker said,

"[We] use the Northern Lights. If you go out with no hat, the Northern Light going to take your head off and use it as a soccer ball."

"We used to be so scared!"

Stories carry a message but intrigue us: we can keep a little distance and absorb information, whereas anger is frightening and direct commands provoke resistance. Not things conducive to learning.

I like Joe's idea that we create our own interesting lives by what we choose to do. I won't be hefting dead beavers into the back of my car any time soon, or sloshing around fields at midnight, I hope. But I'll think about saying yes more often in case there's an adventure I don't know about around the corner.

I'll also mull over what story my local skunks are teaching me, and try to close the cat door earlier in the evening, so I don't end up having a saga to tell about getting sprayed.

## Lifelong Companions

After merely 21 years, I installed new carpeting in my living room. I couldn't afford the bedroom, but that's a much less-traveled thoroughfare, being both private and essentially a cul-de-sac, and also more dimly lit.

The living room is a freeway from front door to back, a dance floor and picnic grounds, a soccer field for cats and friends' children, a zone of refuge for the possums and skunks I'm trying to chase out of the kitchen who turn the wrong way in a panic. When the county widened my road and I found layers of dust inside every kitchen drawer for weeks, some of that grime probably descended into the carpet, too. Staying home during the pandemic's early stages gave me time to notice how revolting it was.

This is not a tragic story. The berber carpet I wanted was less expensive than every other option. The friend who cleans my house lobbied for a darker color, so it will show dirt less easily than the previous one, and I listened to her for once. The carpet layers, John and Larry, hauled my fur-

niture outside for the seven hours it took to do the
job, and then kindly hauled it back in.

What they did not do, however, was pack up
any books. Writers collect books. My bedroom
houses all the poetry and my grandfather's old
Max Brand and Louis L'Amour paperbacks, a copy
of *Frog & Toad*, and some science fiction I don't
want to admit to. But there were three large bookshelves in the living room, housing hundreds of
books. I say "were" because in packing the volumes
into boxes, one of the bookshelves exploded and is
no more. Made mostly of dowels, it was evidently
held together by the weight of the books, as the
glue holding dowels to one-bys had evaporated over
the years. Just after I got the photo albums and
dictionaries off the bottom two shelves, the rest of
the six-foot edifice collapsed.

But as I said, this isn't a tragic story, just a
maddening one. I wasn't planning to go through
my collection and dispense with so much, but it
seemed foolhardy not to, since it had been thrust
under my nose in this way, as if the universe were
making a point. So I dusted off the dead spiders
and let go of my Norwegian textbooks from college,
unopened since then, and the Joan Baez songbook
I learned guitar on in 1968. I gave Andy Goldswor-
thy to an artist friend and *The Birds of Trinidad
and Tobago* to another. My Little Free Library out
by the road is stuffed full and there are boxes on

the ground beneath it, something I'd never let anyone else do, by the way, so don't even think about it.

Someone mentioned that we don't see our books as paper and ink, but as friends or even family: companions who were there with us for specific parts of our lives. No wonder it's hard to let go. Without them, I'm going to have to remember the smell of lilacs in Cambridge myself, unprompted by *Beowulf* or *The Oxford Handbook of American Folklore.* My grandmother's *Home Gardening,* whose print was already too small for me ten years ago, will rest on someone else's shelf. There's such a strange mixture of grief and relief.

Small deaths, perhaps, but we know what they lead to.

## Fathoms

Once you've written 500 radio essays and been applauded for several days, what can you possibly do for an encore? Some things don't have encores, they just continue. Chop wood, carry water. After the ecstasy, the laundry. It was a little awkward that me writing #500 was interrupted by a terrorist invasion of the U.S. Capitol, that threw me off. But I rallied. I'm hoping nothing extreme takes place today. And I don't have anything useful to say about the insurrection, believe me, it's all been said.

One of the difficulties of being a writer these days is how much we're all experiencing the same upheaval. Everyone used to have their particular subjects: water polo, giraffe breeding, Bulgarian movie reviews, climate change. But now we have the same subjects and at the same time, as each new event hits the fan. Plus, all the non-writers take to social media and write about those topics, too. There was so much opinion and personal expression going on when the pandemic started that I couldn't write for months.

I squeezed out a radio essay each week, avoiding current events as much as possible, but no poems got born or were revised. Alone in my house, the public discourse was so fractious and the panic so raw I couldn't even think in sentences. I became monosyllabic just talking to myself.

This is one of the drawbacks of an art form made from the common language. Same reason obstetricians at cocktail parties tell you they're going to write a novel when they retire. I don't go around telling people I'm going to deliver babies when I retire because I never trained in medicine. They haven't trained in writing either, but because we all use the language day in and day out, they feel both competent and entitled. They're wrong, but you can't tell them that, they don't believe it. Far be it from me to tell people not to write, anyway — I've spent much of my life encouraging everyone to write more, because it's good for you. But this year, with the virus, the volume is really deafening.

In local news, right now it's raining. An unforecast quarter inch, at dusk, but it still counts as rain, which we badly need. Apparently no red newts are appearing in this, their season to writhe around on muddy hiking trails in knots and piles of glorious copulation. It's too dry. So, fewer baby newts this year? No newts? And then what? Day after week after mile after acre across the globe, it just grows, the climate crisis. Our crisis.

Everyone I know is hoping fervently that 2021 will be a good year, that last year was just a horrible one-off and there's a way back to what we were used to, what we thought was normal. I don't mean to bum you out, but I think that ship has sailed — it's a delusion to comfort us as we face unfathomable change.

Do you remember what *fathom* means? It's a measurement — originally from fingertip to fingertip when your arms are open wide, but now generalized to six feet. Before the year 1600 it was a synonym for embrace. Then it morphed into a way to measure the depth of water: how many six-feets-es to the bottom of that harbor or this river.

Some water is so deep, though, you can't measure it.

## Cleaning Up My Language

I was just about to say that I hate waiting, but then the word "hate" stopped me. Do I really hate anything? I can get irritated at a moment's notice, and some things — like people running stop signs — are maddening. I certainly feel rage when I'm threatened, and outrage at injustice, but I don't know that I harbor hatred. Not against Mitch McConnell and his greedy disregard for the common good. Not even against the people who raped me when I was a kid.

The older I get, the more curious I am about language. I think the way we use it can change the way we think, and vice versa. It reveals our assumptions and preoccupations. Recently I took the word "lame" out of my vocabulary as a pejorative. Because of the vast consciousness-raising going on in my country right now, it suddenly occurred to me that saying, "Good grief, that is so lame!" would hurt the hearts of people who are actually limping. I'd never say "That is so gay!" or "He throws like a girl!" Sexism and homophobia came to my attention a long time ago.

It took three months of catching myself and reframing sentences before my mind stopped reaching for "lame." Half-way through the process I realized I had another problem: I was turning to slangy words for mental illness as replacements: "That's bonkers" didn't work either. I had to let go of imitating how my Boston cousins in childhood said "That's retahded!" And frankly, this made me sad. I liked saying familiar things from fourth grade like "nutty as a fruitcake," and "bananas up the wall." It was effort to change my habits and I have plenty of other work to do, I didn't need any more.

The thing about consciousness, though, is that once it's been raised, it's very hard to lower it again. When I slipped up and said something was "moronic," it gave me a stomach ache. I really am not in favor of hurting people's feelings or showing disrespect either purposely or out of ignorance. And I'm a writer, for Pete's sake! If using language for the highest good isn't my job, whose would it be?

So I started a list of words I could say that didn't, to my knowledge, rely on denigrating any-one: *amazing, astounding, astonishing, ridiculous, boring, such a surprise, so unlikely. That's effed up, shocking, out of this world.* It feels awkward to use them, but in three months I probably won't notice it was ever an issue. At some point I'm likely to learn more about the world and some of those may have to come out of circulation. The one I wonder about now is "boring." In a way, being charming or entertaining is a privilege and people who don't have those characteristics or social skills might take the word personally. I'm going to need more input on this one, I think. Meanwhile, my ears are open to find neutral terms that express my feelings but respect everyone.

Yes, it's more work. But it's going to save me from needing to apologize to people all the time, whom I didn't even know I was hurting.

And don't you just hate that?

## Mope is a Very Good Word

Well, it's been a quiet week in Nevada City,
my home town. It snowed, that's the big news.
Not the feet everyone predicted, but some lovely
frosted inches. A few schools closed, but not all
of them. Up the hill, though, as we say, where
the interstate barrels over Donner Pass, it was a
white-out and they closed the road for 24 hours so
any eager skiers who weren't already at Heavenly
or Olympic Valley had to stay home and mope.

Isn't "mope" a good word? We don't do enough
moping, in my opinion. We're too busy being
depressed. It's fine to be depressed, don't get me
wrong, we have more than enough reason. But
it's such a boring word, and dreadfully overused.
Much too general. As a poet, I vote for specificity.
Moping seems more temporary than depression
— related to a passing mood instead of something
on-going. When you can't get to the slopes on a
perfect day, you mope. The next day, today in fact,
when the highway is open again and there's still
six feet of fresh powder, you cheer up and hop in
the car without a care in the world.

One might even feel *gleeful* arriving at the lifts,
sun shining, everything whiter than white. No one
uses that word enough either, "glee." If you are
stuck at home, or never did like skiing, maybe take
a minute to spruce up your language. There are
so many great words pining away for lack of expo-
sure. Our homogenized, sound-bite culture goes for
the common denominator, aside from certain weird
fads like "wheelhouse" that pop up now and then.
Why not ditch happy and sad today and instead
feel cheery or glum? Buoyant or doleful? Ticked
or blue? If you're depressed, this will feel like too
much work, but if you're merely moping it might
be a nice distraction.

If you don't know which word would truly describe your feelings, you can always turn to literature for help. Is it an Eeyore mood or more Hamlet? Are you giddy in the way of Eloise at the Plaza
Hotel, or closer to that rascal Peter Pan? This is
a good game for kids, too, if you have any of them
around.

Today, I'm feeling like Paddington Bear: very
lost but outwardly cheerful. I'm trying to figure
out a big decision and have no idea which path to
choose. In reality, I'm so ornery that sitting in a
train station like Paddington with a note pinned
to my jacket saying "Please look after this poet"
probably wouldn't work — I'd just resist attempts
to help me. But it's nice to imagine a day when an-

other person could tell me what to do and I'd agree to do it.

Alas, that is not my fate. My fate is relentless, unending self-determination. Not Paddington, not Hamlet, not even Hagrid and his enormous beasts, because he at least had a job, working for Hogwarts. For me, it's Jo March and the Dread Pirate Roberts all the way.

Sigh.

I'm going to sign off and do some serious moping now. See you later. Have fun if you go skiing.

## True Love

It's windy and rainy and crazy out there, power's out all over the county, but *on* in strange places like three houses including mine and the Willo, the steak house up at the corner of my so-called "block." Trees are down, power poles are askew, and it's Valentine's Day if anyone's paying attention to that, which I am not, being as usual single and less and less affected by manufactured holidays the older I get.

My favorite ex-boyfriend died on February 13th eight years ago, transforming this part of the year into something entirely different for me than a celebration of romance. This is the man I adored but he had a head injury and I finally couldn't marry him and take on the intense caregiving. I put our printed wedding invitations into the recycling one Tuesday morning, back when we didn't have these big lidded containers but only square green uncovered boxes. So I could see them all morning, outside by the curb under the incense cedar, waiting to be taken away. It was April, rather than Valentine's Day, a month before the assigned wedding date. Some images just stick in your mind.

That was the beginning of me waking up from a fog of cultural expectation and looking squarely at love. He and I remained friends for the next 11 years until he died of a heart attack at the house of his next girlfriend. So I didn't see his body or anything. I didn't have to do the funeral stuff, or clean out his tee shirt drawer and take everything to the thrift store. I had already lost him in certain ways, but his death was a huge meteor hitting my planet nonetheless. It shocked me right out of a bad relationship I was clinging to, that was good. And it decimated my idealism about Valentine's Day.

I don't wish you this kind of awakening unless you're seeking it, and who is seeking so much pain on any one day? But it was good for me, later, looking back, to have a true replacement for the hearts and flowers and chocolate. Because I really loved Tad, big time, and I couldn't stay with him even so. Love does not conquer all, in my case. Or love of self conquers love of other, maybe that's more the point. I knew if I married Tad I would turn bitter and eventually mean, and that would not be good for him, or me, or anyone around us. So I had to give up my fondness for the idea of romantic togetherness and not being alone and trudge forth into reality.

Tad loved to say "That's not *my* reality!" whenever one proposed something unpleasant to him: like the necessity of flossing, quitting smoking, or maybe shoveling snow. I loved his ability to fence in his own experience and keep everyone else's out. His head injury made him both extra tender and wildly stubborn, which can be a good combination depending on how you use it. We laughed so much I can still start laughing just thinking about him.

So that's where I go on Valentine's Day: to the stubbornness and tenderness of love, and how it can mow down everything in its path, including romance.

## I Love a Parade

I'm not sure why our town puts up American flags on every lamp post for the Mardi Gras parade, but they do. Oh, wait, no, it was for President's Day! Now I get it. We had intersecting festivities this weekend.

Today is actually Tuesday, though Fat Tuesday was celebrated on Sunday, and the street sweepers are out there washing purple and green glass beads into the gutters under a hundred waving pillow-case-sized flags. It's a little confusing. Not to mention the whole Wash-ington-and-Lincoln-were-born-on-different-days thing.

When I was a kid, there was no school on George Washington's actual birthday, February $22^{nd}$, and the planet turned peacefully on its axis, as it had done since 1879 when the holiday was first invented. We also got a day off on Febru-ary $12^{th}$, Lincoln's day of birth, which I'm sure drove our parents crazy: two holidays in a 10-day window and who's going to babysit? Back then, California, Connecticut, Missouri, and New York had Lincoln's birthday holidays, and of course, Illinois, even though Abe was born, I kid you not, in Kentucky.

Fatefully, if you are still following all this, the Uniform Monday Holiday Act was passed in 1971, when I was almost out of high school, moving Washington's birthday to a day more convenient for parents and other CEOs. Lincoln's birthday got lost in the shuffle until some wily advertising genius coined the term "Presidents' Day" for the third Monday in February, which has never been the official name but persists in public imagination. Now the day is more famous for "white sales," which is something to do with bed sheets, a phrase with so many ironic implications I'm not going to go near it. The only conclusion I can draw is that capitalism once again has taken over common sense and history is being warped as diligently as ever.

Meanwhile, in our town, one that seems to live for parades, we're entering a three-week lull between Mardi Gras and Saint Patrick's Day when the streets will be calm and parking easy to find. Flags tend to stay up for a week past any public event, just to prolong the cheer — it is winter, after all — but they'll come down eventually too, and be packed away in boxes to patiently await Memorial Day, Independence Day, Constitution Day, and finally Veteran's Day in November.

I've always liked the little doodads into which
the flag's dowels are slotted and also the variety
of flags we display: blue and green for the Wild &
Scenic Environmental Film Festival, multi-colored
to announce Hot Summer Nights. I don't go to
every parade, but I appreciate the spirit of celebration around here, and the accompanying props.

Let's get back to reality for half a sec, though,
shall we? Just as George was born on February
$22^{nd}$, not always a Monday, don't forget Mardi Gras
marks the last day of feasting before Lent begins,
a Christian tradition, on Ash Wednesday, 46
days before Easter. It's good to remember, however briefly, what all this folderol comes from and
where it's headed, even if you're a lapsed Unitarian like me and are only in it for the music and the
necklaces.

## Forget About It!

Something my favorite ex-boyfriend Tad used to say all the time was "Not interested!" He had a very deep, gravelly voice and although he could and did talk at great length, believe me, he had a handful of terse statements to spit out like plum pits when he was thinking or reading and didn't want interruptions. I should add that he'd had a head injury in his 20's so many things about him were quirky, to say the least. When I first met him, the finality and speed of those "Not interested!"s shocked me. I come from New Englanders who embroider every sentence with appeals, placations, and outlines of what our reasoning has been to arrive at any conclusion. Our version of "Not interested" is two paragraphs long, accompanied by self-deprecating smiles and suggestions for further conversation.

After I got used to it and realized Tad was being honest and not trying to pick a fight or indicate that he hated me, I grew secretly fond of these pronouncements. *Want to go for a walk? Shall we eat some vegetables for dinner? Hey, let's rent Pride*

& *Prejudice!* "Not interested." I began to use the phrase myself. First just in my head, then as a joke — pitching my voice as low as I could, to sound like him. It made him laugh and laugh.

We lived together for some years and then were dear friends after that, until he died of a heart attack, leaving me to grow older without his company. You probably have lost people in your life, so you know how it is — that the oddest little things come back to you. Tad blooms in my mind sometimes with such strength that I can smell the cigarette on his tweed jacket after he's come inside from smoking half a Camel straight on the front porch.

Over the near-decade without him, I've become less of a placater and self-deprecator and more of a feminist down to my bones, watching how our culture expects women to help and fix and care and put ourselves and our own work aside. Men aren't asked to do this, and in my experience rarely even understand the pressure we endure, nor how hard it is to teach yourself to resist it. I get this, as much as one group can "get" another. This is the same lack of understanding I have about the daily lives of people of color — what their fears may be about violence and othering, about working much harder for things I, as a white person, assume will be easy for everyone.

Last week someone asked me to speak at a meeting for a good cause that I care about. The job came without pay or travel expenses. I could tell she was upset when I turned the offer down, though I explained I'm working on a book with a tight deadline. So I'm not quite there. But one of these days, maybe on Tad's birthday to amuse his ghost, I'm going to open my mouth and tell a complete stranger how I really feel, and not give a hoot about the reaction.

I won't even smile into the telephone when I say: "Not interested!"

### Louis + Dan = Serenity

Between the pandemic and the wildfires
in my part of the world, many of us are quite
frazzled. This is a dignified response, as we say
in life coaching circles. Any reasonable person
would be frazzled trying to cope with the smoke
and the masks-against-smoke worn outdoors, the
masks-against-germs worn indoors, the dangers of
grocery shopping during peak hours, the gloom of
gray skies in very hot weather, having to be in the
house all summer, and so forth. Plus conserving
water, which is olfactorially alarming especially in
the bathroom if you know what I mean. In order
not to completely fall apart, I've discovered two
things to watch on social media.

As you may recall, I am fond of cats. Somewhere along the way, I got tagged and found
myself following a live video feed of a cat named
Louis who lives with his person in the suburbs of
Berlin next to a canal. He's a fluffy striped cat —
what we would call a Maine coon cat in the U.S.,
but the Germans may have a different name for
them. The videos depict the human in her kayak

pulling up to a little dock and Louis jumping in to
sit regally in the prow as he is rowed along in one
direction and then back again. There is, thankful-
ly, no soundtrack, just the slosh of the paddle and
once in a while a brief remark from the person and
very rarely a response from Louis. You can hear
birds and wind in the trees. Sometimes another
kayak goes past, which Louis's eyes follow like a
hawk. That's it. Stultifyingly boring to some of
you, I'm sure, but incredibly restful to me. Eight
minutes of this and I can handle whatever the day
throws at me.

If Louiswildlife (all one word) is not on Facebook, I can turn to Great Lakes Jumper on Instagram to soothe my nerves. Dan O'Conor, a visual
artist who was freaking out a bit, early on in the
pandemic, rode his bicycle down the street to Lake
Michigan and jumped in "in order to clear his
head," he says. The next day he did it again and
has continued up to and including today, through
"snow, rain, and heat" just like that postal carrier
slogan, and sometimes even "gloom of night." His
location is scenic: the Chicago skyline clearly visible in the background and the lake sparkly blue,
cleaned up a lot since I lived there in the 1980s.

Dan's jumps have gone viral and even been covered by *The New York Times*. People travel great
distances in order to join him. His cannonballs are
pretty good, but otherwise he's inelegant, diving

in with bent legs like a frog and often a huge belly
flop, which has got to hurt. Each jump is recorded,
sometimes at normal speed, but often sped up or in
slow-mo, and even to musical accompaniment. He's
a live music fan and began inviting local musicians
to serenade him, since they couldn't play regular
gigs during Covid.

I'm not sure what charms me so much about
these video clips. Their randomness? Their underlying humor? A stout middle-aged man leaping
into cold water and a cat stepping decorously into a
kayak are about as irrelevant as you can get.

And therefore, somehow, magnificent.

## How to Count Flamingos

There is something so unreal about our current situation that I feel it necessary to give you, today, for three minutes, a true distraction. Put all thoughts of illness, droplets, and cabin fever out of your head and pay attention. I'm going to teach you how to count flamingos.

As many of you know, one of my grandmothers was an ornithologist. She had always loved birds and got a banding license back in the days when any backyard birder could get one just by proving they knew a robin from a fire hydrant. Outwardly, she was a wealthy housewife in Buffalo, New York, but inwardly she was a field biologist waiting for the right moment to get to work. Sadly for our family, this happened in 1962, when my grandfather died suddenly and she was widowed. It was especially sad for her, but it also broke her life open. As is sometimes the case, she became a person she would never have been able to be in her marriage.

In 1962 I was seven, and her first grandchild. I lived in San Francisco and she on the East Coast, but through regular letters and summer visits, I became a vessel into which she poured a lot of her wisdom. She always said she'd made a conscious decision, about a year after Papa died, to never say no when someone asked something of her. I think this was her bargain with depression. It also seemed to apply to family members, who were not allowed to resist hanging laundry, but I digress. Thus, when a friend from Fish & Game asked her up in his Cessna to help with the Everglades flamingo count, she said "yes."

Here's what he taught her, she described to me, and I am telling you. To tally flamingos in migration and get anywhere near the right number, you can't count them one at a time. They move too much in flight, one wing looks like another, your neck is craning every which way, peering through the windscreen of the plane, it's just not practical.

So this what you do. Extend your arm out in front of you all the way, palm down. Go ahead. You need to feel this in your body. Fold your fingers into your palm, and stick your thumb out to the side, as if you were hitchhiking, but the back of your hand is facing the ceiling. That thumb is your measuring stick. Now, from the passenger seat of the plane, count how many flamingos are blocked out by your thumb. My grandmother had big hands: her thumb covered ten. While the warden flew neither too close nor too far above them, she looked at the vast moving fields of pink below and counted how many thumbs would cover them all. Then she multiplied by ten.

This wasn't a one-time deal, either. They flew for hours, from one flock to another across southern Florida, and the next day they did it again. She ended up helping them with the count for years.

I hope you'll take this important lesson into your life and use it wisely. You don't even have to be in a plane. It's how I calculate the long vees of Sand Hill cranes as they migrate over my house in October. My thumb covers seven.

I count them, and I wave, just in case my grandmother is up there, watching.

# ARIZONA SUNSHINE
# LEMON PIE

## Jeepers, Creepers

The other night I was sitting on my sofa with
the front door open. I was thinking about masks
and war and human behavior when I noticed there
was kind of a racket going on outside. A big racket.
Then it abruptly stopped. My cat India sauntered
in the front door, and his brother Jack after him.
I said hello in English [*Hello*!] and also in Norwegian [*Hei du*!], as I am encouraging my cats to
become bilingual, and then the racket started up
again. "Wow," I thought, "it's those spring peepers!"

"What the heck are peepers?," you may ask, and
you would be within your rights. I am going to look
this up because I don't know what the heck they
are either. I mean I think they're frogs but why
are they not just called frogs? After a lot of stupid
ads for reading glasses, Professor Google sent me
over to Brian Banbury, a herpetologist who works
for the Ohio Division of Wildlife. "They're small
little frogs," he says, to make sure we understand
the size, "not much bigger than the end of your
thumb." Tree frogs, in fact, who are rather silent
most of the year and not in evidence, although

one famously came in my house all last summer
through the cat door would you believe in order to
reach my kitchen sink. I took him out every evening in my cupped hands. Sometimes he hopped
up and down in there, which is about the weirdest
feeling I know, but often he just waited quietly
until I set him down among the zucchini leaves.

Wikipedia would like to argue with Mr. Banbury,
telling us that peepers are only an Eastern U.S.
resident, and that they are a so-called "chorus
frog." The National Wildlife Federation helpfully
chimes in that they are "about the length of a
paper clip." National Geographic goes one better
and shows us an outline of a peeper next to an outline of a paper clip. How the world can be coming
apart when people are so helpful, I do not know.

No one, it seems, locates any peepers in California, but there I was on my sofa in the Sierra
foothills listening to them live. A Western Chorus
Frog is noted, but its habitat seems to be west of
Pennsylvania and east of the Mississippi, which to
some of us is ridiculous, despite how people on the
Eastern seaboard look at the rest of the country.

I thought peepers were a life stage of froginess,
a teenaged couple of weeks between tadpole and
adult when the hormones ran wild. But that seems
to be something I made up. Peeper is the name
for the entire frog life, or maybe a nickname, after

tree frog, chorus frog, and *Pseudacris crucifer*, the Latin name, which sounds like a rapper to me.

I hope, wherever you live, you will open a window and cock your ears tonight in case some crazy love-struck frogs are in the neighborhood. The noise they make is so hilarious.

Send up a wish, a prayer, a spring peeper chorus for peace while you're at it.

## Sixty-Four

*Note: Earlier in this volume you read about my 65th birthday, and here we have gone back in time to my 64th. I'm sorry, that's just how it goes. I did not promise anyone accurate chronology.*

There certainly are a lot of things I can think of to complain about. I'm thinking of some of them right now, but I'm not typing them out on this page or speaking them into the microphone because I am pretty sure life is too short for complaining. I'm about to turn the age when everyone will sing me a particular Beatles song — you know the one. Don't start yet, though, my birthday isn't until July. I'm getting ready to not complain about that, even though it will be trying to hear it over and over. I've sung it to other people, in my head if not with my actual, literal voice, so I know how tempting it is. We hear this number between one and a hundred and we break into song, like larks in a British hedgerow. You're probably humming it now, in fact. And it's not a horrible song, it's nowhere near as bad as everyone singing you something from Molly Hatchet, for instance, or Celine Dion. It even has two locutions I've always liked: when someone means expensive but they say "dear," and the word "scrimp."

I mean think about *scrimp*: what a great word! The perfect combination of shrimp and cramp, probably from the Swedish *skrumpna*, to shrivel up, to shrink. I love language. I am not complaining about language at all: its strange metamorphoses, the way words hop around from place to place meaning different things. One year cool means sexy and the next year hot means sexy and nobody bats an eyelash about the switch.

Speaking of shrimps, the purchasing of which requires a certain amount of scrimping, I am deathly allergic to crustaceans, so please don't give me any for my birthday. No oysters, lobsters, mussels, clams, or crayfish. In Norwegian, mussels are called "blåskjell" or blue shells, a literalism I adore. The other one I like is moment, which translates to "øyeblikk," or eye blink. Isn't that just superbly obvious?

I'm not sure how we got to Norwegian from complaining, but I'm not complaining. I lived in Norway for one year when I was 21, and learned all about loneliness, waitressing, how to cross country ski down the entire length of a frozen lake all by yourself and not be afraid, and how to have sex in a foreign language. Both sex and foreign languages require a certain proficiency with charades, it turns out, so combining them is not that difficult and sometimes uproariously funny. I will leave this to your imagination.

Norway is northeast of England, where the Beatles grew up, and though I'd like to tell you it's near the Isle of Wight, featured in my soon-to-be-birthday song, it is not — you're thinking of the Shetland Islands, made famous in that mystery series on the BBC where Douglas Henshall stares out across the water. If you listen closely you can hear viewers' hearts break one after another just looking at him. We don't know if he's staring at Norway or the Scottish mainland, but he never complains, despite gruesome crimes being committed all around him and a fairly strange group of castmates.

None of whom, thank heavens, and this is not a complaint, merely a sigh of relief, are named Vera, Chuck, or Dave.

# My Month

April is National Poetry Month and this week I'm in the middle of doing three readings in a row. Tuesday night it was about my latest book: *California Fire & Water, a Climate Crisis Anthology*, and wasn't really a reading but more of a talk about how poetry can help us heal from so many things and also help us manage our fear.

The second, last night, I was one of Five Nevada County Women Poets reading as part of the Sierra Poetry Festival. We've done this every year for the five years of the festival, and especially in this crazy sequestered Covid year it was heartening to see my fellow poets in their little squares on my laptop and hear their new work. Everyone's hair was longer.

Tonight, just as you are listening to this commentary, I'm going to be Zooming down to San Francisco, where I'm part of their One City One Book celebration, reading with another five poets in support of this year's book: Chanel Miller's *Know My Name*. If you don't know her name, think rape, think Stanford a couple of years ago, think general outrage, and if those aren't enough clues please unfriend me on social media, I have no patience any more for people who ignore the on-going fight against male privilege and sexual assault in this century.

I'll be reading poems tonight about my own experience of childhood sexual assault, the family kind, and that's your trigger warning if you need one and were planning to listen. I'm pretty sure the other readers have similar subject matter, and as the organizer, Kim Shuck, says, this reading is going to raise the rafters. April is National Poetry Month and also National Child Abuse Prevention Month. It's kind of my month altogether.

Here's a poem I won't be reading tonight, that is radio-friendly and even mentions God, which is a little strange since I don't technically believe in God, I believe in trees. But God sneaks into my poems now and then, maybe just to prove He or She is all powerful and me being a lapsed Unitarian isn't going to change that.

In any case, remember that I write about many things, including our landscape here in the foothills, and as well as being angry about unfairness and the damage people do to each other, I also at the same time, truly, 24/7, love the world.

## God Speaks to the Rope Swings of Summer

in His gentlest voice, reminding them
about change, about fallow fields and the quiet
everything needs to grow stronger
at facing life and death, uncertainty, joy,
obstruction. This one, hanging straight
from its branch over Oregon Creek, is listening.
He mentions the way opposing twists
will hold each other longer
and how knots keep children's feet
from slipping. Three-ply, four, hemp or nylon,
it doesn't matter. The creek sparkles on.
Woodsmoke dilutes the sky's clear blue.
A madrone leaf slowly spins downstream,
oblivious and holy.

## Arizona Sunshine Lemon Pie

A person could just throw out the three lemons that are beginning to look a little wizened in their blue bowl on the counter. By "throw out," I mean compost. But Antoinette's daughter would have a hard time doing so, not to mention Jonnie's grand-daughter. You don't just fling off the values of your ancestors like a purple wig after Mardi Gras.

Which is why I found myself last Sunday look-ing a little rattled as smoke curled up from the closed oven door. The lemons needing to be used led me to recall an organic pie crust taking up too much room in the freezer, and a recipe I wanted to try involving very little work. You have to de-seed the lemons, but after that they get blended entire with eggs, sugar, butter, and vanilla to make an Arizona Sunshine Lemon Pie. The name was irresistible, and then the lack of zesting. My knuckles and I hate zesting.

As usual, good ideas and good deeds like not wasting three stupid lemons, added to evading hard work a.k.a. zesting, lead to comeuppance, as both Antoinette and Jonnie would have told me.

I am neither a Martha Stewart nor Marie
Kondo type of person. My housekeeping involves
mostly tidy surfaces but Lord only knows what's
going on behind closed doors, including the oven
door, whence was cometh-ing more smoke.

It was almost a warm day, so the front and
back doors were already open. When I cracked the
oven, some convenient breezes blew all the smoke
outside. I turned the appliance off. There was
something unrecognizable smoldering in there, so
I walked out to the deck with a glass of water to
admire my blossoming crab apple for a while and
calm down. The other angle on this event besides
avoiding work involves God — if you believe in God
— perhaps suggesting I could eat less sugar. We
will leave that angle alone. Punitive story-telling
doesn't help anyone.

A few hours later, a friend told me I could learn
to clean ovens on You Tube, so I watched some videos. Baking soda, vinegar, a rag — it didn't sound
too hard and it wasn't, though I had to leave everything in there overnight. More work and mess than
zesting lemons, of course, but you knew that.

I think the smoking culprit was some butter
spilled from the edge of a cheese and onion pie
I'd made the week before. I've lived in this house
with this $300 Sears oven for 22 years and never
cleaned it before. If that appalls you, keep in mind

that it had never smoked before, so didn't really require cleaning. I bake about five times a year.

Antoinette and Jonnie, if they were alive, would laugh very hard at this story and roll their eyes at my lack of expertise, a grown woman not knowing how to clean her own oven being completely ridiculous.

I don't love being the butt of a joke, who does? But I'd be happy to put up with all kinds of ridicule just to see them one more time, standing around in my kitchen with their aprons on, a wooden spoon in my grandmother's hand and a dish towel thrown over my mother's left shoulder.

And the pie, eventually, was delicious. You can look the recipe up on Chef Google.

## Bella Ciao

Last night I stayed up until two in the morning watching "Money Heist," which pretty much ruined today, although I'm not going to admit it. My reflexes are shot, for one thing, and my memory, already disintegrating due to age, is veering around like a drunken swallow looking for its nest under the wrong bridge.

This is no one's fault but my own. I know better than to retire after eleven if I want to enjoy the next day, yet during our endless and maddening pandemic, I stay up late all the time and eat too many chocolate chip cookies while I'm at it. I, who famously didn't have a TV for 20 years and liked the silence, have now watched every detective show set in Finland, Iceland, Sweden, Denmark, and Norway, not to mention England, Scotland, Ireland, and Wales. After searching for something — anything! — decent to view this summer, I even watched Shetland again, including the episode I hadn't liked the first time. Actually, I couldn't remember which episode that was. Watching Douglas Henshall gaze into the empty North Sea is remarkably comforting when the world is coming unglued.

I'd forgotten, in my years of feeling smug that I wasn't addicted to Game of Thrones, that TV is such a great stay against loneliness. There I was on the moral high ground all by myself and the rest of the world was having a good time. This is the problem with smugness, as I'm sure you remember. We feel we've outsmarted everyone else but have merely isolated ourselves.

I returned to "Money Heist" yesterday, having seen the first season and a half and loved it, though it's in Spanish which is too fast a language for me. I quit before the end because I could tell it was going to be tragic and I didn't want to witness that or say goodbye to those savvy gangsters trying to outwit the Madrid police force. Whoever wrote this show was having a truly wonderful time.

This is not a spoiler, though, because the ending didn't happen, Netflix bought the rights and gave them piles of money to film more episodes, which I finally figured out. However, you can only keep hostages at gunpoint and try to extract gold underwater at a fever pitch of tension for so long before it turns into melodrama, and I'm afraid, boredom. When this happens with any show, I listen to the sound but open a new screen and play spider solitaire. This works better in English than in languages I don't speak, like Spanish, since I'm not reading the subtitles, but the music gives you clues about what's going on, and I switch back now and then to not lose the thread entirely.

Apparently the real final actual ending of "Money Heist" will be coming in December. I may have clambered back up to the moral high ground by then, but let's hope not. I recommend it to all you Spanish-speaking, bank-robbing anarchists and other arty types. And if you ever drive past my house after midnight and hear faint gunfire and the song "Bella Ciao," don't worry about me.

I'm just up past my bedtime again, distracting myself from our mutual reality.

## The Lagoon Club

Once upon a time, I lived in a beach town with a lagoon beside it, a big lagoon that separated our town from the next and took 15 minutes to drive around. The road, California State Route 1, was right along the water and the only way out of town northward. In big storms, when it rained for weeks and the tides were extra high, the lagoon tended to flood Rte. 1 and make it impassable. In that sort of weather, often there would be landslides at the other end of town, cutting off Rte 1 from the south so you had to take a mountain road to reach civilization and get gas or go to work. Once, even that road developed slides and we were stuck for a week. California, as perhaps you know, can be quite exciting.

Up here in the Sierra foothills where I now live, six mornings a week I drive to town to get coffee. I can make coffee at home perfectly easily, and far less expensively, but it doesn't taste as good, and I live by myself, work by myself, am constantly by myself. Going to town to stand in a line with other people is important to my mental health. Talking to baristas and friends and strangers makes me feel as though I'm not alone in the world, and also requires I get dressed to face the day. I could be one of those people who stay in their nightgown all day long without proper motivation, and I do not want to find this out.

On the way to town, I take a right off Rte. 49 onto Coyote Street. A patch of gravel, kind of a long curved triangle, has somehow accumulated at this turn-off, I don't know how, and I have to be extra careful to slow down and not let my wheels hit it. This is because I don't want to join The Lagoon Club.

Now mind you, there are no lagoons nearby. But I watched many people in that coastal town join The Lagoon Club. This wasn't the Elks or the Lions, a charitable effort by local citizens. Membership was awarded only to hapless drivers who left Rte. 1 and entered the water, usually because they were going too fast and hit a patch of gravel. Sometimes alcohol was involved, and/or the dark of night. Maybe a deer in the road. The water isn't deep, but it's so muddy you can't drive out again, even if you didn't roll over, and you're up to your doorhandles in salt sea water. A tow-truck has to be called down from Point Reyes, half an hour away, the Volunteer Fire Department comes to save you, trying to hide their grins, and the whole disaster is on everyone's lips by lunch time. Rarely

does anyone get hurt, but the car may not be sal-
vageable. Even the seals, beached on their sand-
bar, will seem to be laughing.

Locals do this as much as tourists, maybe more
— since they know the road so well they're often
speeding. I wasn't around when the Fire Chief's
teenaged daughter, freshly licensed, joined. I hear
it was rather tense. Of course he was worried, but
also he was the one who coined the term, back
in the '60s, and had enjoyed telling stories about
those unlucky drivers ever since.

## Though I Don't Have a Belfry

Unbelievably, it's still National Poetry Month.
If you know any poets, cut them some slack,
they're probably exhausted. I wrote a big grant,
have been part of five readings and one radio show,
and will be included in the Sierra Poetry Festival,
with poets from around the country. The keynote
speaker, Forrest Gander, just happened to receive
the Pulitzer Prize in poetry last week, a lovely
coincidence that makes us look very smart indeed
for inviting him.

Meanwhile, on the home front: the weather
has warmed up, so I'm leaving my back door open
through dusk. Of course a skunk waltzed in the
other night before I'd shut it, and when I spoke
to her sternly, she just kept eating! I got close
enough, stomping my feet for emphasis, that I
could have touched her, and then — a bit startled
— we both retreated. Two hours later I was brush-
ing my teeth and a BAT flew into the bathroom,
circled my head, and zoomed out again. My jaw
dropped, causing a slight waterfall of Tom's of
Maine spearmint foam to descend into the sink. I

had to open the front door in hopes the bat would
exit. I didn't see it leave (I finally had to go to bed)
but I devoutly hope it did. Those guys give me the
willies, even though I respect all living things.

I haven't seen raccoons or possums lately. My
house seems to be a new setting for Wild Kingdom,
but at least not everyone's showing up at once.
Bears open the French doors at my friend Jacquie's
and make a huge mess, eating honey, sugar, crack-
ers, cocoa powder, raisins, and molasses, throwing
sacks of flour around. She's never been home to
witness this, but she sees them padding around
outside on her night camera. The only bear I ever
had walked through the cat fence, knocking it flat,
ate every pear off the tree, pooped an enormous
mound and then clawed through the fence in a
new place to get out. I slept on the deck, oblivious.
My felines were too entranced by the scat pile to
see the fence had been breached, and we patched
it up fast.

A poet's job is to notice things, whether animal,
vegetable, mineral, or abstraction. It's one reason
I like the work — a bat overhead is unnerving but
also something to write about. Thus everything
can be used: it's a perfect closed loop of recycling!
I don't, of course, write about all of it. Topics can
be too personal to share, or another person's story
to tell. Some are deeply boring. But I use quite a
bit, as you may have noticed: possums and skunks,

a dicey childhood, flat tires, one-night stands, the fierce green of buckeye leaves unfurling in spring.

I didn't plan to be a poet, any more than I planned to hang around skunks. It just kind of happened and I rolled with it. Poetry saved my sanity and gave me a new language. Skunks, so far, are teaching me to not be afraid. And they're a great model of persistence.

I hope I don't have to learn some darn lesson about fumigation, though. I'll keep you posted.

## A Whale Story

Since poetry is not exactly lucrative, most
of my poet friends have other jobs. One is a
whale-watching guide off the coast of Cape Cod
in Massachusetts and recently posted a photo of a
Fin Whale on social media — something I'd never
heard of. There was nothing but blue ocean for
scale, so I asked her how large it was. "They're
small in the North Atlantic," she said. "This one
was about 60 feet long."

Now in some ways, I am both a visual person and smart, but measurements have always
escaped me. Friends tell me that things are two
football fields long, as if that will help. It does not
help. When faced with distance, I do one of two
things: try to remember what it feels like to stand
in my 10' by 12' writing studio and then multi-
ply, or imagine my college friend Brian Guffrey,
who is 6'3", lying down over and over across the
required space. This doesn't work because after
four Guffreys my perspective gets foreshortened,
but it's always amusing to try. Brian was my first
tall male friend and I had a massive crush on him

for quite a while. I hope he would like knowing I've been using him as a yardstick since 1973.

I received the Fin Whale post while I was sitting in my favorite corner of the long, rectangular café I frequent. I tried laying imaginary Brian Guffreys along its speckled concrete floor and got half-way to the bakery case before giving up. A young family was at the next table and I asked both parents — because I am an equal-opportunity questioner — if they were good at measuring distances. The woman blanched but the man said, "Yeah, I can try."

"How long is this restaurant?"

He looked down to the far end by the bathrooms and and then up at the ceiling for some reason, which is at least two Guffreys high and decked with home-made prayer flags. He took his time, possibly doing math in his head not related to 6-foot-3-inch units. "I'd say 55 feet," he said.

My eyes widened and I told them about the 60-foot whale and showed their kids the photo. Five more feet added to this café lands us half-way into their woodshed but it's a measurement I can remember, especially when looking at the outside from across the parking lot. Now, however, I'm going to have to go look up how tall Fin Whales are, to really understand the size.

The morals of this story are, of course, to stay curious, to ask for help from strangers, to always share photos of whales with children, and to find

interesting ways to remember the friends you
made in college even when you haven't seen them
since your mother's funeral 22 years ago.

If you need further marine inspiration, follow
this whale-watching poet on Instagram at e.brad-
field. If you need more practical life hacks, you can
find me at the end table in what I now, secretly,
am calling The Fin Whale Café.

## My Real Name

When I get an e-mail that starts "Dear Mary Fisk," I erase it without reading the rest. My legal name is Mary Elizabeth, but my parents called me Molly at birth and people who use Mary on me are almost always trying to sell something. When I get a call from a number I can't recognize, I don't pick up the receiver. 98% of the time, whichever robot it is doesn't leave a message.

This modern world brings us a huge amount of stupid new work avoiding the global advertising machine. It's a huge pain in the saucepan. I am not selling my house, dear unknown realtor, nor do I have anything to invest, Ms. broker from Iowa, and heaven help me, Harvard University, you already have so much money it's just impertinent for you to ask for any of mine.

One reason to take time off from electronics is to recall those good old days back in 2003 when few people asked anything of you. You could just exist. Try it! Turn your ringers off, and see if you can go a whole day without any magic machinery. If a neighbor comes over to borrow sugar, that will

be entertaining rather than an annoyance. You can
ask what the sugar's for, and vote for no walnuts
in the chocolate chip cookies if you're asked. You
might even get one later, or three, as interest on
your loan. After the beeps and pings are stilled,
your ears will once again hear amazing things like
birdsong, traffic, cat snores, and wind in the highest branches of the pines. This is quite restful, it
turns out, because you don't have to defend yourself against it. You can let it wash over you like
warm water, or music.

I'm not going to ditch my laptop and phone:
they're vastly useful. But the assault of ads and
spam and unlooked for communication that de-
mands instant response is wearing out our nerve
endings. It's leaving us less fit for larger endeav-
ors, like addressing the climate crisis and closing
down U.S. Border concentration camps. Whether
that's by design or not I'll leave to you to decide.

People like to think about history as being either horrific or quaint. What they don't tend to remember is that it was true. There really were a lot
of horses in the world in 1905, which meant livery
stables, saddle makers, anvils, rope, and hay — all
kinds of horse-related circumstances. I'm not trying to go back in time: using a buggy would drive
me insane. It's just worth thinking of what we gain
and lose with innovation, and paying attention,

looking beyond the convenience and excitement of the new tools.

Advertising harassment is an electronic-related circumstance, and I am really sick of it. My house and car and purse used to be private space. Now a bunch of greedy strangers keep showing up there without asking and I have to spend precious time throwing them out. It's maddening, and exhausting. I'm not sure what to do about it, yet, but I'm going to do something. Anyway, that's my rant for today. Fie upon you, commercial hyenas!

And don't call me Mary Elizabeth, either.

## Stubbornest

I'm thinking about the human impulse to name
things, and know the names of things. There's
a mountain peak I see whenever I drive up over
Donner Pass to Lake Tahoe, and every single
time I say to myself: *I wonder what that's called?*
I've been told its name, but just like the exact
elevation of Donner Pass, which is over 7000 feet
and also a palindrome, giving me two of the four
numbers, I can't seem to remember it.

I used to name my cars. The red and white '69
VW bus that stalled out on the highway every
time I drove to Vermont was called Alice. But
subsequent rides devolved to the Dasher Wagon
and the Planet Jetta. After I finally figured out
that Volkswagens had to be repaired too often
and Toyotas did not, I dropped the manufacturers
names, too.

One line of thought says naming things is
a way to claim them. If you call it Castle Peak
instead of "third mountain on the left," you're
more involved. And of course if you name it after
yourself or your favorite president, there's an

assumption of possession. The land I live on, which is mostly owned by Bank of America, is unceded by the local native Nisenan tribe. I refer to it as the Poem Farm with mixed feelings, thinking I should learn the Nisenan name and also probably give it back to them.

Robert Hass, a poet I love, once wrote: "Of all the laws that bind us to the past, the names of things are stubbornest." I can still remember how proud I was of learning to spell our street name when I was a kid: Divisadero. Between that and San Francisco, I felt glad to be from where I was from so I knew how to spell those hard words early on. I thought it gave me an advantage in facing other life difficulties. Mind you, I was six. When I hear the street on the news, I can see it: a silver ribbon extending from the Bay all the way to Market Street. It is mine the way the whole city is mine 53 years after we moved, the way California remained mine when I lived in Boston, Norway, and Chicago.

But it's not that I own these places, it's that I belong to them. They own me, if you will. My skin wakes up in a primal way at the smell of eucalyptus cloaked in fog or the cable car's chime even in a stupid TV ad. Every lighthouse is the Alcatraz light hitting my bedroom window.

As I write this, I can feel language receding and my senses coming forward. The names are

meaningful to me, but it's the sensory response to
where I am that carries real power. Because we're
animals in the end. We managed without words for
a long time and that memory lives in our cells. The
names of things may be stubbornest, as Hass says,
but what we experience is most essential: Salt
air, the sun on our faces, and the cries of whatever those birds are — the ones we don't know the
names of — right where we're standing.

## Name That Season

For about two weeks every spring, my part of
the world becomes fluffy. This may not be a strictly
scientific term to describe foothill riparian habitat, so if you're a field biologist or some kind of
arbor professional, please forgive me. But visually,
through the eyes of poets, painters, and school children, everything looks fluffy. The bare branches of
fruit trees have already blossomed and leafed out.
The oaks — blue, black, valley, etc. — all turned
their startling neon green and then moved into a
full summer hue that's darker and more dignified.
Now the last deciduous leaves have appeared and
are in a pale, transitional state — cottonwoods,
maples, Littleleaf lindens, ashes and alders — a
tender array of color that softens town and highway, both.

It won't last. Nothing lasts. But for about ten
days, it's magic. There ought to be many more
names for seasons than the usual four. Spring
alone has at least five stages, including this one.
And it would be fun to give them all names, in case
"fluffy" doesn't do it for you.

These are the things a person might think
about after a hernia operation, when she is allowed
to drive again but can't walk very far yet, so toot-
les around in her car early on a Saturday morning
just to get out of the darn house and see what has
changed while she was sleeping and eating Sal-
tines.

I will not bore you with stories of bad reactions
to anesthesia or hydrocodone, nor will I name the
friends who saved my hide, again, because I don't
want you to steal them. Someone who holds a
plastic waste basket under your chin without being
asked is not for sale.

Town was gorgeous. The farmers were just
setting up their Market, boxes of produce all over
the place and trucks akimbo. No tourists on the
sidewalk yet, with or without their masks. I went
on a route I never take, up above Brunswick to
see what all that new construction is about — you
can only glimpse it from the freeway — noting
how many cars were in line at the just-completed
Dutch Brothers Coffee that will likely put two local
cafés out of business: 43 cars. Then I took the back
road to our local upscale campground in case there
were any Airstreams I needed to oogle. Oogling
Airstreams I will never own and probably wouldn't
like living in is my forté. They are so sleek. As
opposed to, for instance, fluffy, the state of our

foliage, as I mentioned. Today, no Airstreams but a nice brown dog to whom I waved.

My bandage from the operation was between me and the steering wheel, cleverly never getting caught as I turned the wheel right and then left, so I admired that dance for a moment. Heading back to the main part of town, almost finished with a cup of coffee, I passed our very old but newly re-modeled hotel, The National, its balcony gleaming with new paint. *That might be a good spot to write poems this summer*, I said to myself, out loud. And then: *I think that's enough scenery for one day.*

When you're an invalid, and also a grown-up, and it's the weekend, nine o'clock in the morning is not too early to go home for a nap.

## Peaches, Prunes & Alfalfa

I am teaching on Zoom during whatever we're
calling this long home stay. I teach cancer pa-
tients, their caregivers, and family members and
the way I do this is to offer up writing prompts.
Every Thursday morning you will find me — it
used to be in a café but now I do this on my sofa
— wracking my brains to think up eight or nine
prompts for the class that afternoon. Last week
I asked them what they had learned while se-
questering at home. One took herself in hand and
studied all she could about Zoom. She has a green
screen and everything! Another is practicing not
getting rattled about lack of productivity. Many
are making food they haven't cooked in years. My
student with the wonderful Dutch accent under
perfect English rediscovered that a good hard
walk does indeed cure bad moods.

So far, my biggest revelation is that you can
buy bales of hay on the telephone. I thought
hay was one of those things you had to get in
person at a feed store, having already borrowed
somebody's truck and possibly dressed for the

occasion. This is one reason I've never bought it before: I don't have the right clothes. Also, I heard there was hay and straw and one was better than the other but I didn't know which. I hate feeling dumb and unprepared, don't you? Not knowing what I would need for mulch, or what to do with it once it was in my yard made me cranky. Even reading Gary Snyder's poem about haying didn't help.

Luckily, I was saved by a book. On page 137 it said that alfalfa hay was a good mulch as it is full of nitrogen and protozoa. It does have seeds (I know some of you are hollering into your radios about the seeds), but fewer than other kinds of hay, and when you mulch thickly the weeds that grow up are easy to pluck out.

As we are not allowed to gallivant in stores, I still felt a little stymied, but then I remembered a place called Ridge Feed. I once stopped by there on a whim to visit baby chicks. I thought hay might be a subset of "feed," and I was right!

Who knew you could call and get one bale of alfalfa hay brought to your house? You don't even have to wear overalls to take delivery. I'm not sure how I'm going to pull the hay apart, since it's roped up and prickly, but I'm hoping the book will tell me, or else Farmer Google. I am not unintrepid and I'm sure those people upset about the alfalfa seeds are going to show up and help me figure this out.

My only previous connection to alfalfa was in the sixth grade when S. told us about the different kinds of kissing. She was very advanced. In case you missed this lesson, kissing can be divided into three words that help you make your lips adopt the shape for each method. Those words are *peaches*, *prunes*, and *alfalfa*. We of course whooped with laughter at that last one and didn't believe a word of it.

You think I'm going to close without telling you the book's name, don't you?

Of course not. It's called *Grow Your Soil!* by Diane Miessler.

## Skunk Farts

At 4:00 this morning, I was awakened by the smell of skunk. I rolled out of bed and stood up, my brain evaluating the situation. Not a big, close, or recent spraying. Faint but unmistakeable.

The sound of un-cat-like chewing came from the kitchen. I can't describe cat-like chewing, but when it's not a cat, it's obvious. Possums chew as if they're breaking up individual food pellets with a hammer. Skunks chew fast and in bursts, with more of a *chip* than a *chomp* sound, like a kid might eat an ear of corn if he'd lost his two front teeth and had to use his incisors.

My skunk persuasion tactic is to shuffle into the kitchen, scuffing my feet so it doesn't get startled, and keep up a friendly monologue about how skunks live outdoors and it's time to go home now, this is not your house, etc. I am finally smart enough to put the cat food bowls away at night, but some people — I'm looking at you, India, cat of great appetite and un-slender-ness — demand treats and then abandon a few on the floor. The skunks are grateful. I am less so.

As I've reported before, often skunks hear me coming and turn left to hide under my grandmother's hutch. This is not ideal, but at least it's so low under there they can't stand up, which is the only way they spray. This seemed to be a new skunk. He didn't leave immediately, but when he finally saw me and zipped over to the cat door, his tail was much fluffier than any others I've seen. He bolted, the fine aroma of his ilk wafting gently behind him.

As it was still the middle of the night, I opened the back door and locked the cat door. I can't do this all night because my cats want to go in and out. When they can't, they wake me up. This is not acceptable, as I'm sure you understand. India and Mimi just *meow* severely, but Jack, if he can't budge me by staring from two inches away or pawing my face, jumps onto my bureau and whacks the necklaces hanging on the wall. For some reason this sound has me on my feet in seconds, fully adrenalized. It isn't valuable jewelry, and none of it would break if it fell. I don't know why this acts on my brain like a baby's cry acts on a parent. And how did Jack discover it worked so well? He isn't a wise cat, but he's canny. Street smart. In the movies, he would be played by Robert Downey, Jr. He's the one who figured out if you catch a gopher you should eat it in the bathtub because it won't be able to escape up those smooth porcelain sides, and now they all do it.

I went back to bed. A scrabbling sound was heard from the deck. I ignored it. It persisted. The skunk was trying to dislodge the cat door's lock. These cat treats are like crack cocaine. I lay in bed wondering if my patience would outlast the skunk's determination and then I must have fallen asleep, because I woke to my alarm at 7:00 from a dream of looking up whether skunks fart or not.

I actually did look it up, and Professor Google says yes.

# Acknowledgements

Each essay was originally aired as radio commentary on KVMR's News Hour. "Praying for Possums," commentary #384, was also included in *Houston, We Have a Possum*.

Unlike my earliest essay books, funded by day jobs and loans from friends, *Everything But the Kitchen Skunk* was made possible through the financial contributions of my patrons, both private and those on the arts-funding platform Patreon. I'm a long-time fan of crowd-sourcing for many reasons, especially how direct it is: the connection between people is immediate and personal, uninterrupted by bureaucracy. I support many artists this way, as well as people in crisis. I think it's an effective, egalitarian way to strengthen community as well as a lovely way to support the arts.

To be on the receiving end of this support has meant the world to me and has expanded my creativity in all kinds of ways. I'm so grateful to my current and past patrons, who include:

Ellen Aisenbrey, Jennifer Andaluz, Ruth Bavetta, Lindy Beatie, Dan Bellm, Kaby Birdsall, Eileen Blodgett, Juliet Bradley, Katy Brown, Sue Brusseau, Nancy Jean Burns, Sheila Cameron, Laura Cherry, Randy & Katie Chilton, Karen Donaldson, Janet Delgado, Kay Drake, Brion & Alice Dunbar, Caitlin Featherstone, Joanie Ferenbach, Judith Fenzi, Sarah Fisk, Andrea Frankel, Sandy Frizzell, Pascal Fusshoeller, Kimberlee Gerstmann, Sarah Griscom, Jan Haag, Eileen Hale, Robert Lee Haycock, Shawna Hein, Willow Hein, Judith Hill-Weld, Sharon Hollis, Jackleen Holton, Joanna Howard, June Hymas, Deborah Jacobs, Pati Johnson, Maxima Kahn, Katherine, Keri Kemble, Julia Kelliher, Ellen Kelman, Debra Kiva, Marilyn & Bob Kriegel, John Lace, Devi Laskar, Helen Lay, Jennifer Long, Deborah Lopez, Pamela Mack, Lisa Majaj, Robin Mallery, Jennifer Mary, Joan Mazza, Sarah Miller, Claudia Mills, Talei Hoblitzell Mistron, Catherine Montague, Anita Montero, Kim Musillani, Jude O'Nym, Teri Orr, Sara Oseasohn, Theresa Pappas, Nynke Passi, Missy Patton, Charlotte Peterson, John Schelling Pollock, Andie Pope, Erica Randall, Joanna Robinson, Lenore

Rosenberg, Suzi Schell, Shannon Francis Schott, Sandra Scott, Serticans, Nancy Shanteau, Janeen Singer, Ann Smith, Katherine Smith-Schad, Jinny St. Goar, Catherine Stifter, Deb Stone, Carol Tahir, Theresa Thomas, Sabrina Thompson, Marcus Thomson, Doug Vandiford, Teresa Wann, Denise Wey, Kimberly Williams, Trixie Wilson, Susanna Wilson, Nancie Laird Young, Cheryl Zatuchni, and many who prefer to remain anonymous.
*www.patreon.com/MollyFisk*

## About the Author

Molly Fisk is the author of the essay collections *Naming Your Teeth; Houston, We Have a Possum; Using Your Turn Signal Promotes World Peace;* and *Blow-Drying a Chicken*, and the poetry collections *The More Difficult Beauty; Listening to Winter; Terrain* (co-author); and *Salt Water Poems*. She edited the climate crisis poetry anthology *California Fire & Water* with a grant from the Academy of American Poets. Her essays have aired weekly as part of the News Hour of KVMR-FM Nevada City, CA since 2005.

Fisk is the Inaugural Poet Laureate Emerita of Nevada County, California, and has been awarded grants by the Academy of American Poets, the National Endowment for the Arts, the California Arts Council, and the Corporation for Public Broadcasting. She works as a radical life coach in the Skills for Change tradition and is fond of open water swimming where there are no sharks. Visit her at mollyfisk.com.